Welcome to My World

Exploring the lives of children in Ethiopia, India, Peru and Vietnam

DVD and activity pack for primary teachers

By Emma Wellsted and Dan Cook

Young Lives
An International Study of Childhood Poverty

Save the Children

Save the Children fights for children in the UK and around the world who suffer from poverty, disease, injustice and violence. We work with them to find lifelong answers to the problems they face.

www.savethechildren.org.uk

The Young Lives project is studying the lives of 12,000 poor children in Ethiopia, India, Peru and Vietnam – 3,000 children in each country. It is an innovative longitudinal investigation into the changing nature of childhood poverty in the selected countries and seeks to contribute to a broader understanding of poverty reduction policy, knowledge and reforms. It reflects a holistic understanding of childhood poverty that incorporates economic, social, physical and demographic indicators of childhood well-being.

Young Lives will continue to monitor the well-being of the children involved up to 2015, in line with the year the Millennium Development Goals will be evaluated. These eight goals, agreed at the New York Millennium Summit in 2000, aim to work towards the development of the whole world and thereby eliminate global poverty.

Young Lives is a partnership between the University of Oxford, other UK universities, Save the Children and prominent national research, policy and governmental institutes in the four study countries. The project is funded by the UK Department for International Development (DFID) for the benefit of developing countries. The views expressed here are not necessarily those of DFID.

www.younglives.org.uk

The Geographical Association is a subject association with a mission to further the learning and teaching of geography. Its membership of approximately 7,000 includes teachers in primary and secondary schools and further education, academic geographers and teacher educators and trainers.

The Association crosses academic communities and promotes the development of global sensitivity and understanding through 'thinking geographically'. The Geographical Association is happy to support the Young Lives project and to have the opportunity to show the inherent geography underpinning the understanding of childhood poverty.

Emma Wellsted is a geography teacher and principal author of *Welcome to My World*.
Dan Cook is a primary teacher. Both live in Reading.

Acknowledgements

Thanks to: Anna Lawrence, Radstock County Primary School, Wokingham; Judith Enang, Upcroft Primary School, Reading; Louise Parr, Whitehall Primary School, Uxbridge; Lorraine Wadsworth, St Margaret's School, Hampstead; Julie Price and Sandra Evans, Barley V C First School, Royston; Teresa Devlin, Banbridge Integrated Primary School, Banbridge; the Geographical Association's Early Years and Primary Phase Committee; and Sue Jagelman and Rosemary Mallard.

Published by
Save the Children
1 St John's Lane
London EC1M 4AR
UK

First published 2007

© The Save the Children Fund 2007
Registered Charity No. 213890

ISBN 978 1 84187 113 4

Design of inside pages: Neil Adams
Illustrations: Bethan Matthews
Photographs: Jaime Razuri; Aida Ashenafi, Mango plc; Michael Monteiro; Ly Thai Dzung

Printed by Page Bros

Contents

1 Notes for teachers

Aims of the pack

Welcome to My World provides information, activities and materials to enable pupils to explore the lives of four children selected from four developing countries: Vietnam, India, Ethiopia and Peru. The ten activities in the pack provide pupils with the opportunity to:

- investigate similarities and differences between pupils' lives and the lives of the four selected children
- examine a locality in a less economically developed country
- explore a number of geographical issues
- explore aspects of citizenship and PSHE
- gain an understanding of what it is like to live in poverty and explore the opportunities and problems young people encounter
- generate discussion about development issues and ways that children's lives can be improved
- enhance literacy and numeracy skills in an engaging context
- focus on ideas for further engagement and fundraising.

Learning about the lives of children in these countries helps pupils to:

- develop as 'global citizens' by equipping them with skills to make informed decisions and take responsible action
- make links between local and global issues and understand the global context of their local links
- critically examine their own values and attitudes
- appreciate similarities between peoples everywhere
- value diversity and understand the importance of respecting differences in culture, customs and traditions
- develop skills that will enable them to combat injustice, prejudice and discrimination
- appreciate the links between the lives of others and their own lives
- understand how people can improve the environment or damage it and how decisions about places and environments affect the future and quality of people's lives.

Taken from *Developing the Global Dimension in the School Curriculum*, DFES, 2005

For a fuller discussion of teaching geography and the global dimension at primary level, see Young, M (2004) 'Geography and the global dimension', in S Scoffham (ed.) *Primary Geography Handbook*, Geographical Association, Sheffield, pp 217–227.

Using the pack

What's in the pack?

Pupil activities comprise the main body of the pack. The activities aim to give pupils an understanding of:
- the lives of the four children in the case studies
- relevant geographical topics – migration, rural and urban living, and development issues
- aspects of citizenship and PSHE.

The activities are supported by:
- a DVD containing short films
- country profiles (page 16)
- children's stories (page 26).

The glossary of terms (Appendix 2) gives definitions of key terms that appear in the activities. Each activity lists words the teacher may find it useful to go through or to display in a prominent place in the classroom before the lesson starts.

Some activities have an information box for teachers (marked *i*), providing additional background information.

The activities are divided into six sections, with one or two activities in each section. The first section introduces the four children and the countries they live in. Each of the following four sections explores the life of one child and focuses on a particular theme: growing up in the countryside, moving to the city, keeping healthy and going to school. The final section explores ways that children in the UK can get involved.

Most activities start with a section called 'let's start with me'. This introduces the geographical issue that the activity explores and allows pupils to consider aspects of their own lives before they go on to explore children's lives in other countries.

Approximate timings for the activities are indicated in the top right-hand corner of the activities. They allow for discussion time. For early finishers or upper key stage 2 pupils, extension activities are suggested.

Differentiated resources for some activities are available for lower key stage 2 pupils or for use with lower ability pupils within an upper key stage 2 classroom. Suggestions for how to use these resources are given in the instructions to each activity.

Films on the DVD

There are four short films on the DVD (4–6 minutes each), one for each child, to introduce them to pupils. When showing one of these films it is important to stress the similarities in young people's lives, as well as differences. For example, look for similarities in the rhythm of children's lives – time to play, time for school – and with hobbies, ambitions, relationships between brothers and sisters, etc. The activities give guidance on which film to use and when. See Appendix 1 for a transcript of the films.

Country profiles and children's stories

The country profiles (page 16) give key information on the four countries the case study children come from, plus the UK to allow comparison. The children's stories contain key information about each child's life: their home and family, their neighbourhood, and their day. The instructions to the activities suggest ways to use the profiles of the four countries and children's stories.

World map

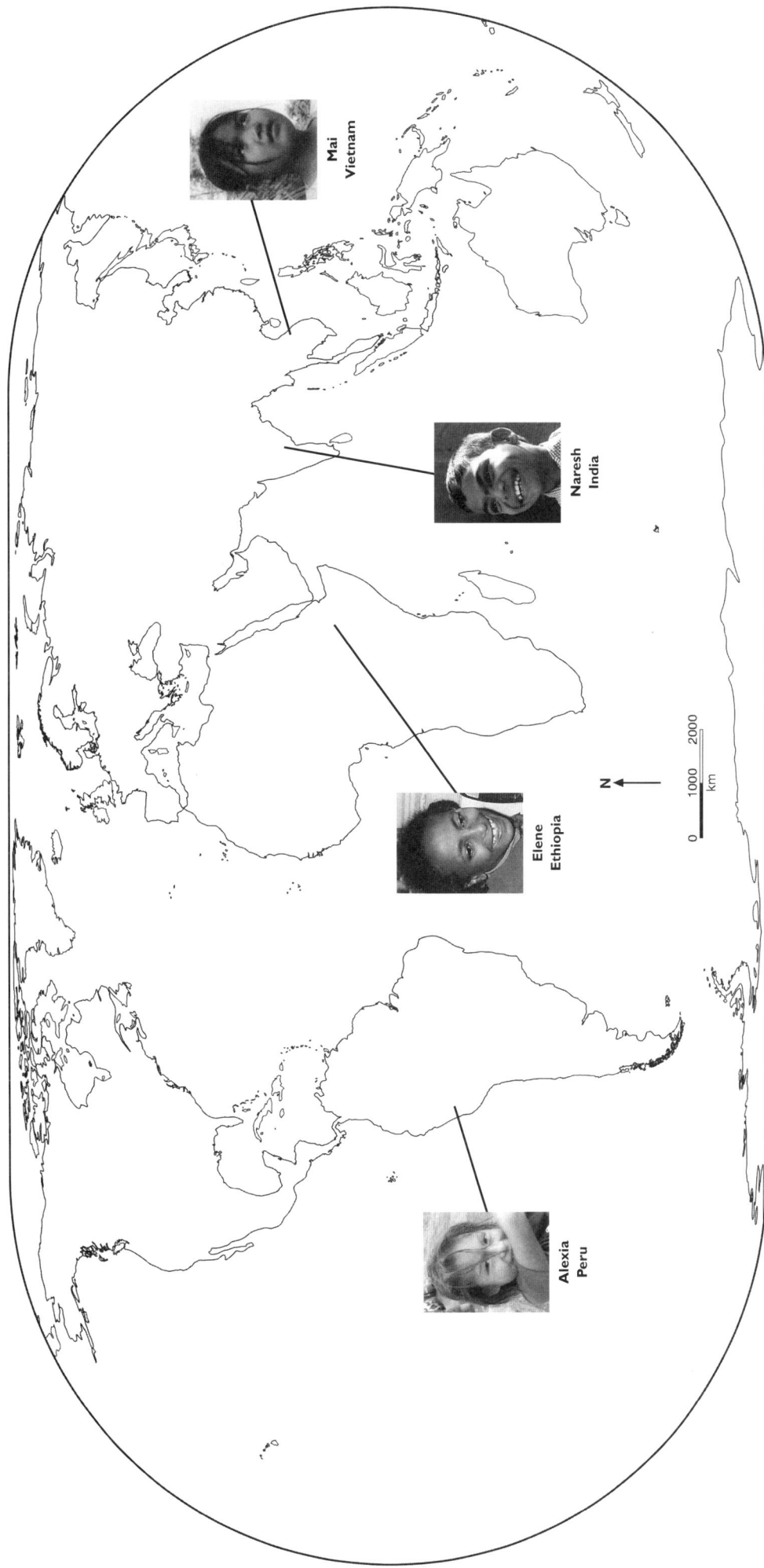

Mai
Vietnam

Naresh
India

Elene
Ethiopia

Alexia
Peru

N

0   1000   2000
km

Young Lives
An International Study of Childhood Poverty

Save the Children

2 Curriculum coverage

England: curriculum links for geography, citizenship/PSHE, literacy and numeracy

Geography curriculum: Key Stage 2

Undertaking geographical enquiry: *Pupils have opportunities to:*
1a. ask geographical questions
1b. collect and record evidence
1c. analyse evidence and draw conclusions
1d. identify and explain different views that people, including themselves, hold about geographical issues
1e. communicate in ways appropriate to the task and audience
Developing geographical skills: *Pupils have opportunities to:*
2a. use appropriate geographical vocabulary
2c. use atlases, globes, maps and plans at a range of scales
2d. use secondary sources of information
2e. draw plans and maps at a range of scales
2f. use ICT to help in geographical investigations
2g. develop decision-making skills
Knowledge and understanding of places: *Pupils have opportunities to:*
3a. identify and describe what places are like
3b. understand the location of places and environments they study and other significant places and environments
3c. describe where places are
3d. explain why places are like they are
3e. identify how and why places change
3f. describe and explain how and why places are similar to and different from other places in the same country and elsewhere in the world
3g. recognise how places fit within a wider geographical context
Knowledge and understanding of patterns and processes: *Pupils have opportunities to:*
4a. recognise and explain patterns made by individual physical and human features in the environment
4b. recognise some physical and human processes and explain how these can cause changes in places and environments
Knowledge and understanding of environmental change and sustainable development: *Pupils have opportunities to:*
5a. recognise how people can improve or damage the environment and how decisions about places and environments affect the future quality of people's lives
5b. recognise how and why people may seek to manage environments sustainably, and to identify opportunities for their own involvement
Study of localities and three themes: *Pupils have opportunities to study:*
6a. a locality in the United Kingdom
6b. a locality in a country that is less economically developed
6d. how settlements differ and change, including why they differ in size and character and an issue arising from changes in land
6e. an environmental issue, caused by change in an environment and attempts to manage the environment sustainably

Through studying countries and themes, the *Welcome to My World* scheme of work offers opportunities to study at a range of scales – local, regional and national – and to study a range of places and environments in different parts of the world, including the United Kingdom (7b).

Activity number

1	2	3	4	5	6	7	8	9	10

1	2	3	4	5	6	7	8	9	10
●		●	●				●	●	
●		●							
●	●	●	●	●	●	●	●	●	●
		●	●			●	●	●	
●						●	●	●	

1	2	3	4	5	6	7	8	9	10
●		●	●			●	●	●	
●					●	●			●
●	●	●	●	●	●	●	●	●	●
				●	●				
●		●					●		
●		●	●		●	●			

1	2	3	4	5	6	7	8	9	10
●	●	●	●	●	●	●	●		
●	●				●	●			●
●						●			●
				●	●	●	●		
		●				●			●
	●	●	●	●	●		●		
		●	●						

1	2	3	4	5	6	7	8	9	10
			●						
			●					●	●

1	2	3	4	5	6	7	8	9	10
		●				●		●	●
		●			●	●			●

1	2	3	4	5	6	7	8	9	10
●	●	●	●	●	●	●	●	●	●
	●	●	●	●	●	●	●		●

England: curriculum links

continued

In many primary schools, QCA schemes of work are used to deliver geography in Key Stage 2. The table opposite shows how the *Welcome to My World* pack covers each and every learning objective of the QCA schemes of work units 9, 10, 15 and 24. The *Welcome to My World* pack can be used in conjunction with, or replace, these existing QCA schemes of work without major disruption to existing long-term plans.

QCA Curriculum Links: Geography

QCA Unit 9: Village settlers (Yr 4) *Children should learn:*
to investigate places
to ask geographical questions
about the characteristics of settlements
to use a key to interpret symbols
to recognise that most places are connected to others
to recognise that settlements have specific features
to draw a map of the layout of a settlement
QCA Unit 10: A village in India (Yr 4) *Children should learn:*
to respond to geographical questions
to use and interpret globes, atlases and maps
to investigate places
to use secondary sources
to use ICT to access information
how places relate to each other
to make maps
to identify main physical and human features
about similarities and differences between places
to identify land use
to begin to understand the relationship between location and economic activity
how places relate to each other
QCA Unit 24: Passport to the World (Yr 1–6) *Children should learn:*
to investigate places
to collect information
to use secondary sources
to record and present information
to analyse evidence
about current affairs to recognise and investigate places
to identify the location of different places in the world
QCA Unit 15: A mountain environment (Yr 6) *Children should learn:*
about different types of environments
about the world distribution of environments
to use globes and atlases
to use ICT to access information
to use secondary sources
how the environment affects the nature of human activity

Activity number

1	2	3	4	5	6	7	8	9	10

1	2	3	4	5	6	7	8	9	10
●	●	●	●	●	●	●	●	●	●
●		●	●				●	●	
●	●	●	●	●	●	●	●		
					●				
		●	●						
●	●		●		●				
				●	●				

1	2	3	4	5	6	7	8	9	10
●		●	●				●	●	
●					●	●			●
●	●	●	●	●	●	●	●	●	●
●	●	●	●	●	●	●	●	●	●
●		●					●		
		●	●						
				●	●				
			●						
	●	●	●	●	●		●		
			●		●				
			●						
		●	●						

1	2	3	4	5	6	7	8	9	10
●	●	●	●	●	●	●	●	●	●
●		●							
●	●	●	●	●	●	●	●	●	●
●						●	●	●	
●	●	●	●	●	●	●	●	●	●
		●	●						●
●	●				●	●			●

1	2	3	4	5	6	7	8	9	10
●	●				●	●			●
●	●				●	●			●
●					●	●			●
●		●					●		
●	●	●	●	●	●	●	●	●	●
			●		●				

England: curriculum links
continued

Citizenship/PSHE curriculum: Key Stage 2

Developing confidence and responsibility and making the most of their abilities *Pupils should be given opportunities:*
1a. to talk and write about their opinions, and explain their views, on issues that affect themselves and society
Preparing to play an active role as citizens *Pupils should be given opportunities:*
2a. to research, discuss and debate topical issues, problems and events
2c. to reflect on spiritual, moral, social and cultural issues, using imagination to understand other people's experiences
2e. to recognise the role of voluntary, community and pressure groups
Developing good relationships and respecting the differences between people *Pupils should be given opportunities:*
4b. to think about the lives of people living in other places and times, and people with different values and customs
4d. to understand that differences and similarities between people arise from a number of factors, including cultural, ethnic, racial and religious diversity, gender and disability
Knowledge, skills and understanding *Pupils should be given opportunities:*
5b. to participate

Literacy and numeracy links

Literacy
Numeracy

Activity number

1	2	3	4	5	6	7	8	9	10
								●	
		●	●			●		●	
	●	●			●	●	●	●	
		●							●
●	●	●	●	●	●	●	●	●	●
●				●				●	
		●							●

Activity number

1	2	3	4	5	6	7	8	9	10
●	●	●	●	●	●	●	●	●	●
●				●					

Wales: curriculum links

Using geographical enquiry and skills, the *Welcome to My World* scheme of work offers opportunities to study at a range of scales – local, regional and national – and to study a range of places and environments in different parts of the world, including the United Kingdom.

Geography curriculum: Key Stage 2

Geographical enquiry and skills *Pupils have opportunities to:*
1. observe and ask questions
2. collect, record and present evidence to answer questions
3. analyse evidence and draw conclusions
4. use and extend geographical vocabulary
7. make and use maps and plans at a variety of scales
8. identify and locate places using atlases
9. use secondary sources for information
10. use ICT to gain access to additional information sources and assist in handling, classifying and presenting evidence
2. Places *Pupils have opportunities to study:*
1. where the locality is and how it links to other localities
2. what the locality is like and what geographical patterns can be identified
3. why the locality is like this and what processes are contributing to its development
4. how it compares with other places and what are the similarities and differences
5. why people's views differ about how the locality is changing
7. interrelationships within the wider world in terms of decision-making and global citizenship
3. Themes *Pupils should be taught to:*
1. identify ways in which people affect the environment
2. investigate ways in which people attempt to achieve sustainable development
3. recognise that people have different views about changes made to the environment
Pupils have opportunities to:
4. begin formulating ideas and opinions about geographical issues and events
5. understand the individual's responsibility for the environment

Activity number

1	2	3	4	5	6	7	8	9	10
●		●	●				●	●	
●		●							
●	●	●	●	●	●	●	●	●	●
●		●	●			●	●	●	
●					●	●			●
●									
●	●	●	●	●	●	●	●	●	●
●		●					●		
●	●	●	●		●	●			●
	●	●	●	●	●		●		
		●				●			●
	●	●	●	●	●		●		
					●	●			
●		●				●			
		●	●		●	●			●
		●				●			●
					●	●			●
		●	●	●	●	●		●	●
						●			●

Wales: curriculum links *continued*

PSE curriculum: Key Stage 2

Attitudes and values *PSE provision should enable pupils to:*
take an active interest in the life of the community and be concerned about the wider environment
Skills *PSE provision should enable pupils to:*
listen carefully, question and respond to others
express their views confidently and take part in a debate
empathise with others' experiences and feelings
be still and reflect
develop decision-making skills
work co-operatively to tackle problems
Knowledge and understanding *Pupils should:*
know how the environment can be affected by human activity

Northern Ireland: curriculum links

Teachers in Northern Ireland will find that activities in this resource pack offer many opportunities for children to explore children's rights globally while developing literacy and numeracy skills. The activities will be particularly relevant to the 'World Around Us' area of learning, and also provide ways for children to practise thinking and ICT skills. This pack is targeted at Key Stage 2, but might be useful for pupils in Primary 3 and 4, as they begin to explore how other children live in different places.

Activity number

1	2	3	4	5	6	7	8	9	10
●	●	●	●	●	●	●	●	●	●
●	●	●	●	●	●	●	●	●	●
●	●	●	●	●	●	●	●	●	●
●	●	●	●	●	●	●	●	●	●
●	●	●	●	●	●	●	●	●	●
●		●	●		●	●			
●		●	●	●		●	●	●	●
		●	●	●	●	●			●

Scotland: curriculum links

Environmental Studies 5–14 National Guidelines
Social studies

People and Place Levels B and C *Pupils are able to:*
identify places using maps and globes
describe main features of maps
describe main features of their Scottish settlement
compare their Scottish settlement with others
compare and contrast their daily routine with children elsewhere
give reasons why life differs in different parts of the world
describe main features of some common types of land use
People and Society Levels B and C *Pupils are able to:*
give examples of some needs of different types of people
identify some of the rights and responsibilities children have
describe ways people can participate in the decision-making process

Education for Citizenship in Scotland
(Learning and teaching Scotland audit materials)

Citizenship audit areas *Knowledge and understanding of:*
contemporary social and cultural issues
individual and social needs
decision-making processes
Skills in:
working in teams to carry out tasks
communicating effectively with others
researching and handling information
thinking critically about evidence
Values, including dispositions to:
respect self and others
share responsibility for community welfare
value and respect cultural and community diversity
understand and value social justice
Creativity and Enterprise, including encouragement to:
develop independent thought
define problems and suggest how to work through solutions
use creative forms of self-expression
observe and reflect on their social, natural and made environments

Activity number

1	2	3	4	5	6	7	8	9	10
●					●	●			●
					●				
	●		●	●	●		●		
	●		●	●	●		●		
●	●		●	●	●		●	●	
	●	●	●	●	●		●	●	●
			●	●					
●	●			●				●	●
					●	●			●
		●							●

Activity number

1	2	3	4	5	6	7	8	9	10
	●	●	●	●	●	●	●	●	●
	●	●	●	●	●	●	●	●	●
●		●	●		●	●			
●		●	●	●		●			●
●	●	●	●	●	●	●	●	●	●
●	●	●	●						●
●		●				●		●	●
●	●	●	●	●	●	●	●	●	●
		●							●
●	●	●	●	●	●	●	●	●	●
		●		●		●			●
●	●	●	●	●	●	●	●	●	●
					●	●			●
								●	●
			●	●	●				

3 Country profiles

Vietnam

Some information about Vietnam

The capital city of Vietnam is Hanoi.

The main language spoken is Vietnamese. English is becoming popular and increasingly favoured as a second language.

The currency is the dong (£1 = 30,000 dong).

80% of the population have no religion, 9% are Buddhist, 7% are Catholic, and 3% are classed as having other religions.

Vietnam has a population of 80.2 million people. Of these, 30.7 million are under the age of 18. This means that for every ten people, three or four are children.

People can expect to live until they are **71 years old**.

66% of people are farmers. This means that for every ten people, six or seven are farmers.

96% of children go to primary school. This means that for every ten children, nine or ten go to school.

90% of adults can read and write. This means that for every ten adults, nine of them can read and write.

26% of people live in towns and cities. This means that for every ten people, two or three of them live in cities.

18% of people live on less than $1 per day (about 60p). This is described as living in absolute poverty. This means that for every ten people, one or two of them live in absolute poverty.

Vietnam

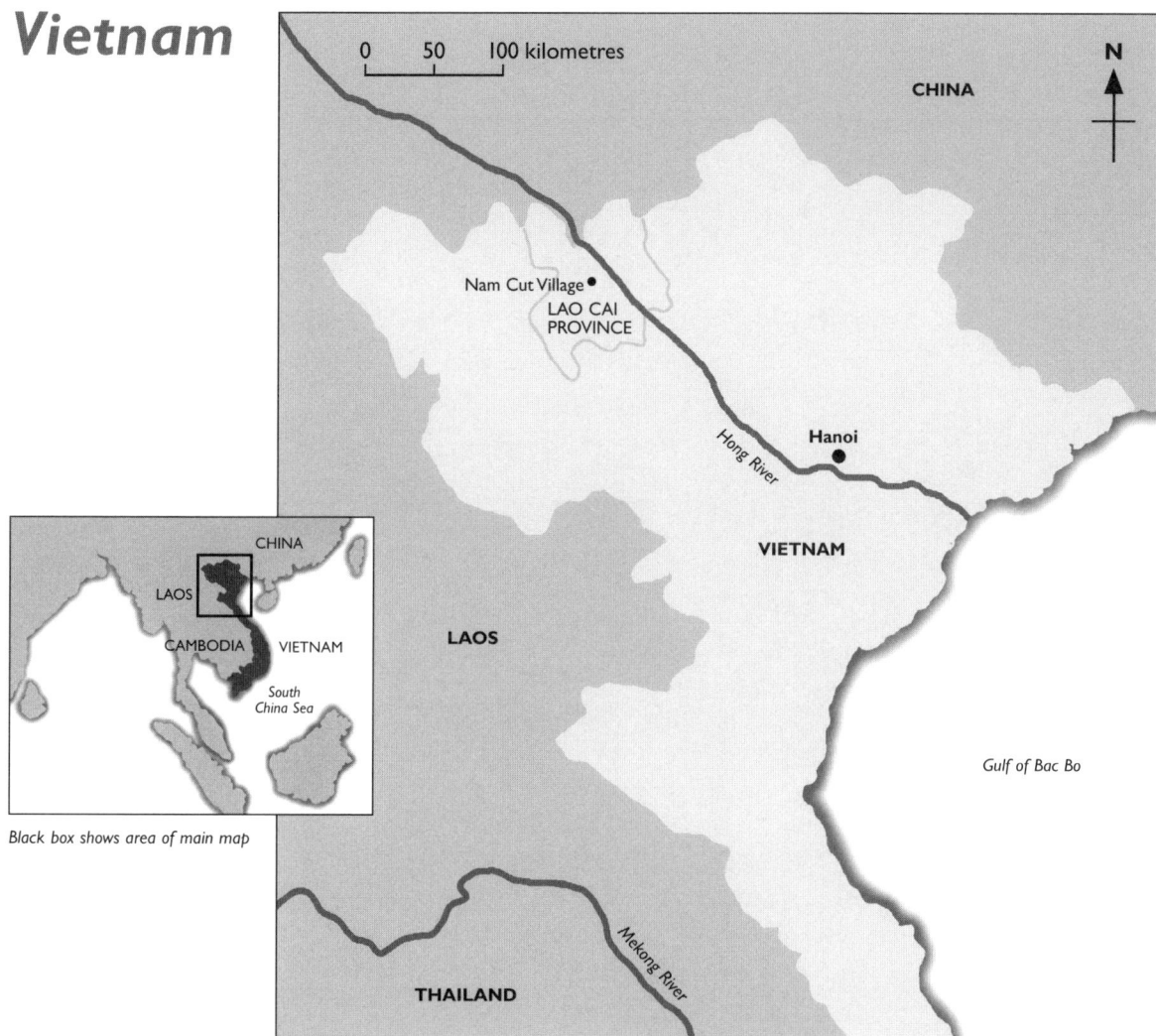

Black box shows area of main map

The climate of Cao Bang, north Vietnam

Month	J	F	M	A	M	J	J	A	S	O	N	D
Average rainfall (mm)	25	32	38	89	165	197	191	193	114	64	38	13
Average maximum temperature (°C)	9	8	18	23	28	29	30	29	29	26	22	16

Sources: Statistics from *The State of the World's Children*, UNICEF 2004 (accessed via www.unicef.org.uk) and *The World Factbook* (accessed via www.cia.gov); BBC Weather Information (accessed via www.bbc.co.uk/weather)

India

Some information about India

The capital city of India is New Delhi. However, India is a diverse country that is made up of 28 states and seven union territories.* Andhra Pradesh, where Naresh is from, is one state in India. It is the fourth largest state by area and has the fifth largest population. It is the largest and most populous state in southern India. The capital of Andhra Pradesh is Hyderabad.

The currency is the rupee (£1 = 85 rupees).

81% of the population are Hindu, 13% Muslim, 2% Christian, 2% Sikh, and 2% are classed as having other religions.

Hindi is the national language spoken by 30% of the people but there are other official languages spoken, including Bengali, Telugu and Gujarati.

India has a population of 1.04 billion (1,049 million) people. Of these, 419.4 million are children. This means that for every ten people, around four are children.

People can expect to live until they are **64 years old**.

66% of people are farmers. This means that for every ten people, six or seven are farmers.

77% of children go to primary school. This means that for every ten children, seven or eight go to school.

61% of adults can read and write. This means that for every ten people, six or seven of them can read and write.

28% of people live in towns and cities. This means that for every ten people, two or three of them live in cities.

35% of people live on less than $1 per day (about 60p). This is described as living in absolute poverty. This means that for every ten people, three or four of them live in absolute poverty.

*A union territory is an administrative division of India. Unlike states, which have their own local governments, union territories are ruled directly by the national government.

India

MAHARASHTRA

INDIA

CHATTISGARH

Black box shows area of main map

THE HIMALAYAS

CHINA

PAKISTAN

NEPAL

BANGLADESH

INDIA

Andhra Pradesh

SRI LANKA

Indian Ocean

● Hyderabad

ANDHRA PRADESH

KARNATAKA

Krishna River

N

Bay of Bengal

0   50   100 kilometres

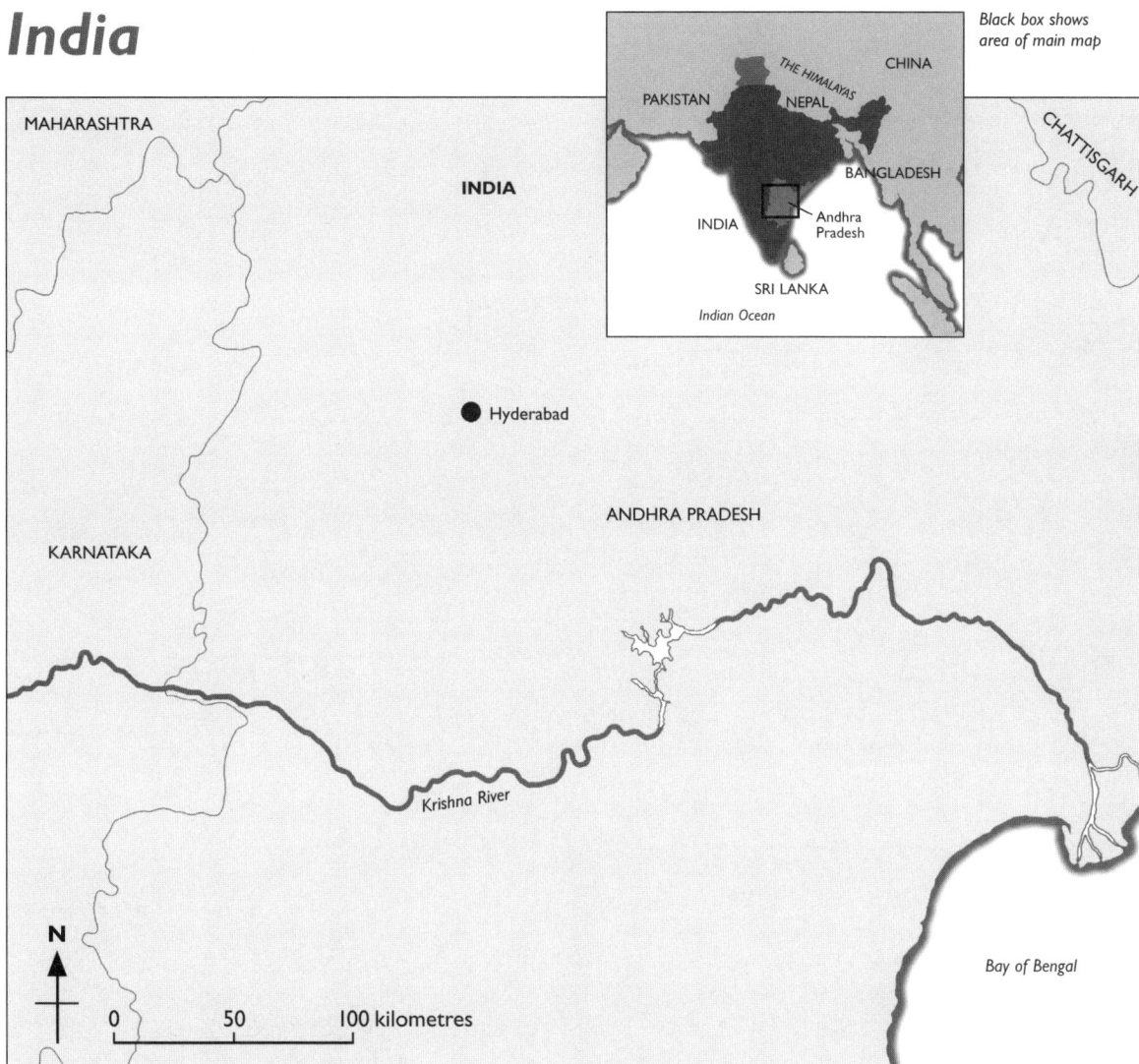

The climate of Hyderabad, Andhra Pradesh, India

Month	J	F	M	A	M	J	J	A	S	O	N	D
Average rainfall (mm)	8	10	13	31	28	112	152	135	165	64	28	8
Average maximum temperature (°C)	29	32	36	38	40	35	31	31	31	31	29	28

Sources: Statistics from *The State of the World's Children*, UNICEF 2004 (accessed via www.unicef.org.uk) and *The World Factbook* (accessed via www.cia.gov); BBC Weather Information (accessed via www.bbc.co.uk/weather)

Ethiopia

Some information about Ethiopia

The capital city of Ethiopia is Addis Ababa.

The main languages spoken are Amharic, Tigrinya, Oromigna, Guaragigna, Somali and Arabic. English is the major foreign language taught in schools.

The currency is the birr (£1 = 17 birr).

45% of the population are Muslim, 35% Ethiopian Orthodox Christians, 12% animists, and 8% are classed as having other religions.

Ethiopia has a population of 68.9 million people. Of these, 39 million are under the age of 18. This means that for every ten people, five or six are children.

People can expect to live until they are **48 years old**.

85% of people are farmers. This means that for every ten people, eight or nine are farmers.

31% of children go to primary school. This means that for every ten children, three or four go to school.

39% of adults can read and write. This means that for every ten people, three or four of them can read and write.

16% of people live in towns and cities. This means that for every ten people, one or two live in cities.

82% of people live on less than $1 per day (about 60p). This is described as living in absolute poverty. This means that for every ten people, eight or nine of them live in absolute poverty.

Ethiopia

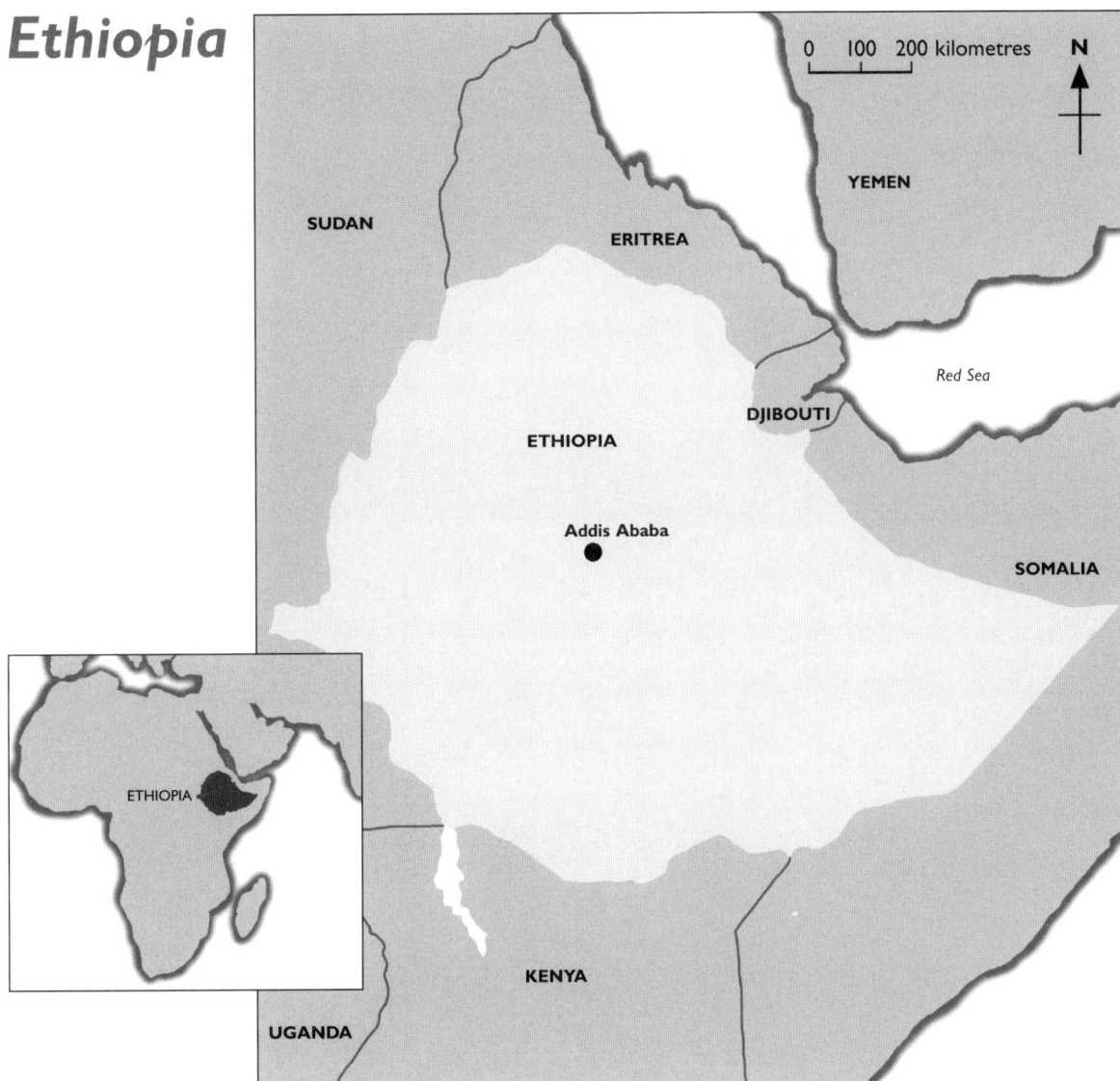

The climate of Addis Ababa, Ethiopia

Month	J	F	M	A	M	J	J	A	S	O	N	D
Average rainfall (mm)	13	38	66	86	86	137	279	300	191	20	15	5
Average maximum temperature (°C)	24	24	25	25	25	23	21	21	22	24	23	23

Sources: Statistics from *The State of the World's Children*, UNICEF 2004 (accessed via www.unicef.org.uk) and *The World Factbook* (accessed via www.cia.gov); BBC Weather Information (accessed via www.bbc.co.uk/weather)

Peru

Some information about Peru

The capital city of Peru is Lima.

The currency is the nuevo soles (£1 = 7 nuevo soles).

Spanish is the official language spoken but Quechua and Aymara are also spoken.

81% of the population are Catholic, 2% Christian, and 17% are classed as having unspecified religions.

Peru has a population of 26.7 million people. Of these, 10.7 million are under the age of 18. This means that for every ten people, four are children.

People can expect to live until they are **70 years old**.

9% of people are farmers. This means that for every ten people, around one of them is a farmer.

96% of children go to primary school. This means that for every ten children, nine or ten go to school.

88% of adults can read and write. This means that for every ten people, eight or nine of them can read and write.

74% of people live in towns and cities. This means that for every ten people, seven or eight of them live in cities.

16% of people live on less than $1 per day (about 60p). This is described as living in absolute poverty. This means that for every ten people, one or two of them live in absolute poverty.

Peru

BOLIVIA

PERU

Bajo Chavini •

Ene River

THE ANDES

● Lima

COLOMBIA
ECUADOR
PERU
BRAZIL
BOLIVIA
CHILE

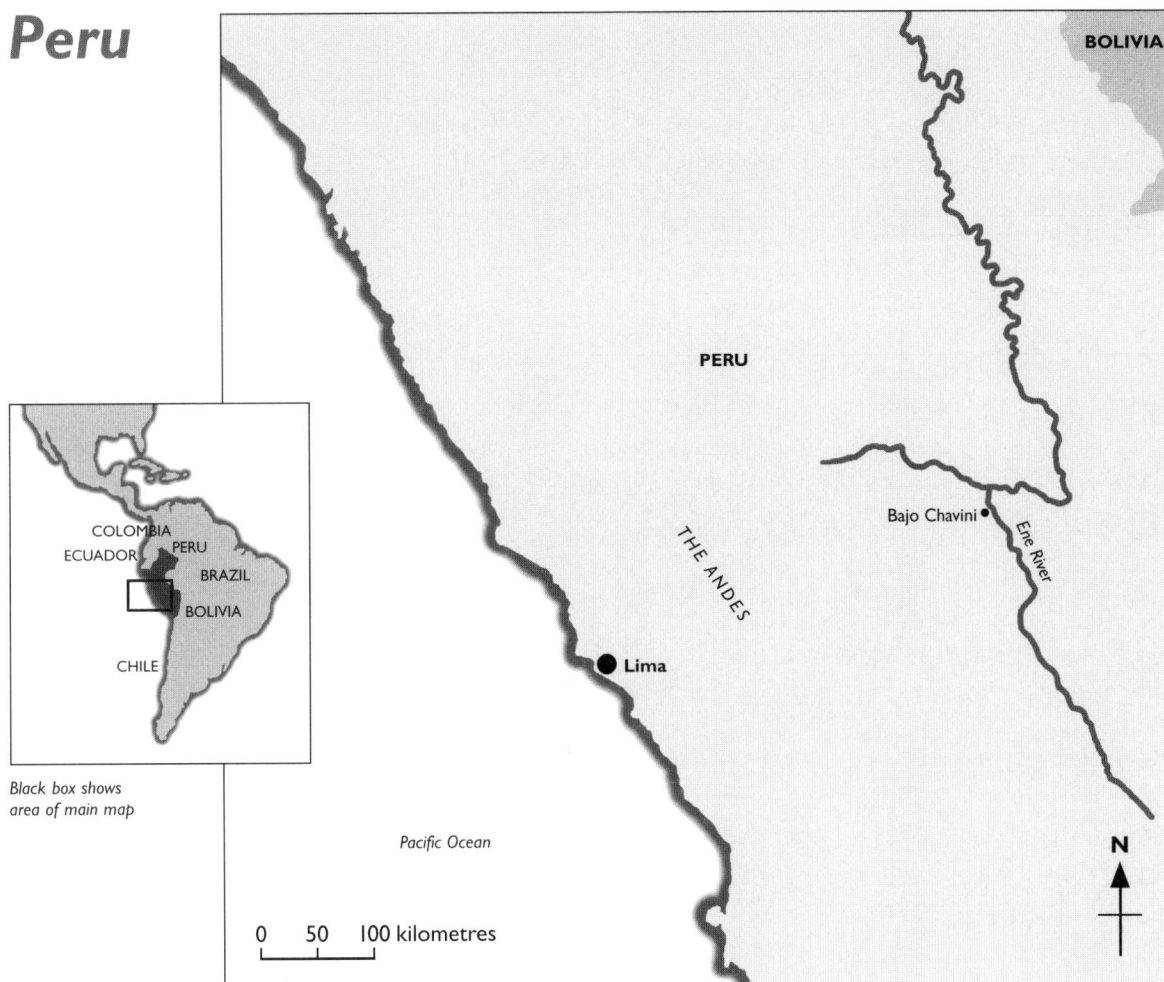

Black box shows
area of main map

Pacific Ocean

N

0   50   100 kilometres

The climate of Lima, Peru

Month	J	F	M	A	M	J	J	A	S	O	N	D
Average rainfall (mm)	3	0	0	0	5	5	8	8	8	3	3	0
Average maximum temperature (°C)	28	28	28	27	23	20	19	19	20	22	23	26

Sources: Statistics from *The State of the World's Children*, UNICEF 2004 (accessed via www.unicef.org.uk) and *The World Factbook* (accessed via www.cia.gov); BBC Weather Information (accessed via www.bbc.co.uk/weather)

Country profile: UK

Some information about the UK

The capital city of the UK is London.

The currency is the pound.

The major language spoken is English. 26% of the population of Wales speak Welsh.

71% of the population are Christian, 3% Muslim, 1% Hindu, 1% are classed as other, and 23% are classed as having no religion.

The UK has a population of 59 million people. Of these, 13.2 million are under the age of 18. This means that for every ten people, two or three are children.

People can expect to live until they are **78 years old**.

1.5% of people are employed in agriculture (farming). This means that for every ten people, less than one is a farmer. However, farming uses 75% of the nation's land.

99% of children go to primary school. This means that for every ten children, nine or ten of them go to school.

99% of adults can read and write. This means that for every ten people, nine or ten of them can read and write.

90% of people live in towns and cities. This means that for every ten people, nine of them live in cities.

0% of people live on less than $1 per day (about 60p). This is described as living in absolute poverty. This means that for every ten people, none of them live in absolute poverty.

UK

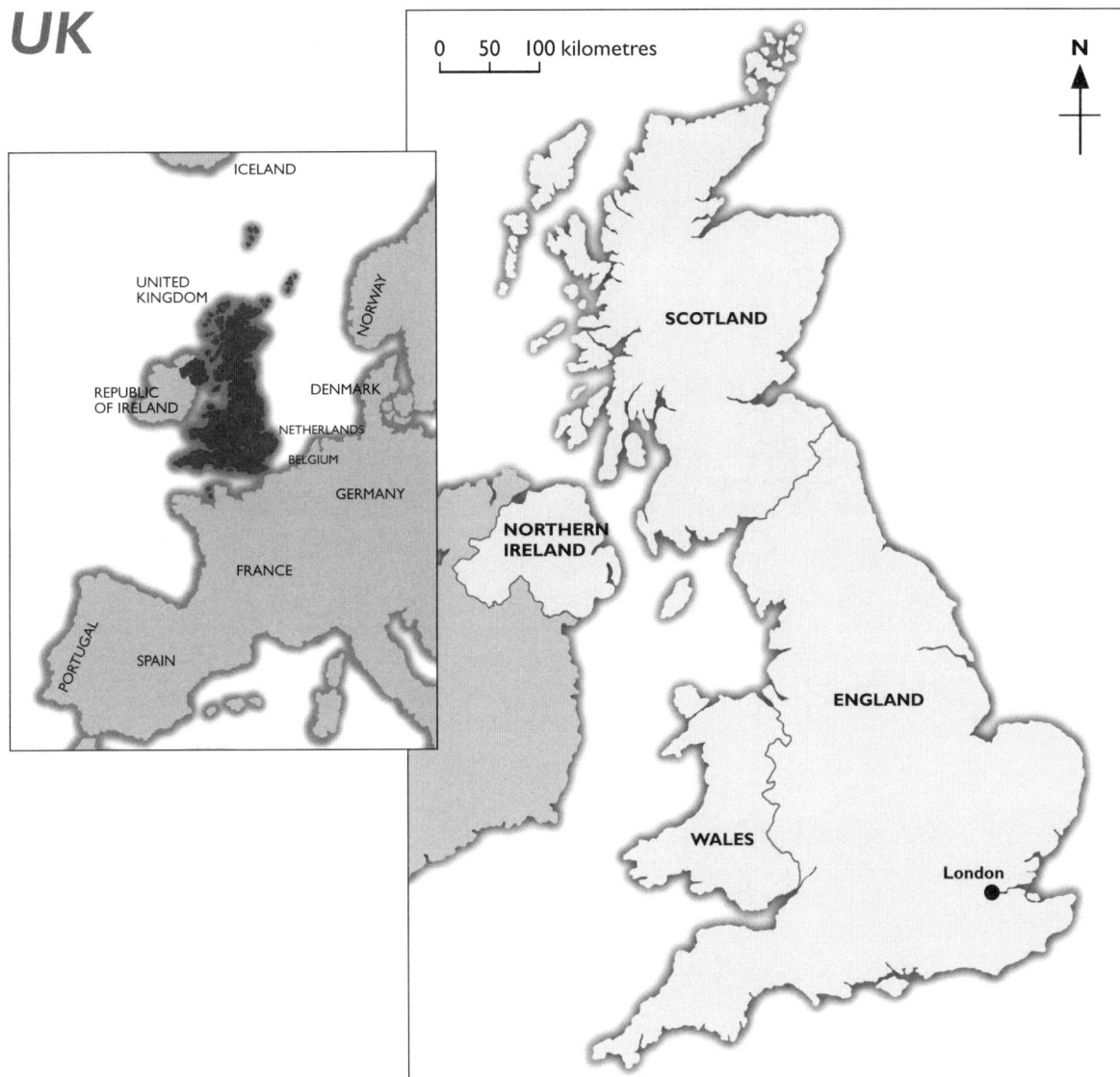

0   50   100 kilometres

N

ICELAND

UNITED
KINGDOM

NORWAY

DENMARK

REPUBLIC
OF IRELAND

NETHERLANDS

BELGIUM

GERMANY

FRANCE

PORTUGAL

SPAIN

SCOTLAND

NORTHERN
IRELAND

ENGLAND

WALES

London

The climate of London, UK

Month	J	F	M	A	M	J	J	A	S	O	N	D
Average rainfall (mm)	54	40	37	37	46	45	57	59	49	57	64	48
Average maximum temperature (°C)	6	7	10	13	17	20	22	21	19	14	10	7

Sources: Statistics from *The State of the World's Children*, UNICEF 2004 (accessed
via www.unicef.org.uk) and *The World Factbook* (accessed via www.cia.gov);
BBC Weather Information (accessed via www.bbc.co.uk/weather)

4 Children's stories

Meet Mai, 10, from Vietnam

Mai lives in a poor and remote mountain village in rural Vietnam.

Mai's home and family

Mai lives in Nam Cut village, which is a poor and remote village in Lao Cai Province. She lives with her mother, father, grandfather, grandmother, sister and brother. Mai's family earns money through farming and keeping animals such as pigs, chickens and a cow. They grow sugar cane and corn on their land behind their house and a small amount of rice. They also buy food.

They live together in a small, one-roomed wooden house with a side section used for storage and cleaning. The floor is stone and the roof is cement and bamboo. The small concrete yard in front of the house is normally covered in dried vegetable peel for the chickens to graze on. There is also a separate thatched hut to the side of the house, which is the kitchen. This has a fire fuelled by bamboo, which they collect from the nearby forest. A water pump sits behind the yard, where they get their drinking and washing water from. The family has a small colour TV.

The main room has two beds, two long benches and a table in the middle, made by Mai's father, Doan Van Tho, who is a carpenter. Her parents are also farmers. Tho taught himself carpentry and makes furniture for friends and family. The money from the carpentry pays for his children's food and education but he could make more money if he moved away from the village to work. He does not want to do this as he does not want to leave his family.

Mai's neighbourhood

Mai's village does not have many people living there. It is hard to reach the village as it is in a mountainous area. The steep mountains are hard to farm and the weather is often very cold and wet in winter.

Mai's day

Every day, Mai wakes up at 5.30am. She checks her homework from the previous night. She has a breakfast of rice and sometimes vegetables. At 7.30am she walks to school, which is 1km away. Children who live further away often cycle.

Mai is in the fourth grade and only wears uniform on a Monday, which is a formal school day. The uniform is blue trousers and a white shirt, with a red neckerchief. The school has four main buildings with a large schoolyard in the middle. Every morning a drum is beaten to signal the beginning of school and the children line up in the yard. Mai studies literature, science, maths, Kinh (the local language), art, history, geography, ethics, PE, grammar and music. Mai's favourite games to play with her friends are hide-and-seek and blindfolded catch.

Mai's school finishes at 11am. She goes home and normally makes lunch – rice and vegetables. She then looks after her younger brother so that her parents can work in the fields surrounding the village. After lunch she sleeps for one hour and then, at 1.30pm, she goes to work in her family's rice fields until 5.30pm. She either grazes the cows or leads the buffalo around the field to tread the rice.

Mai helps her mother, Bich, and grandmother cook the evening meal. They usually eat tofu, rice and vegetables. They don't eat much meat as it is too expensive. After dinner Mai does her homework, then goes to bed at 9pm. Mai wants to complete her schooling all the way to upper high school (14 or 15 years old). "When I grow up I want to be a doctor as I want to help other people in my village," she says.

Meet Naresh, 9, from India

Naresh lives in the city of Hyderabad in India. Many people who live here have migrated (moved) from their villages in the countryside because they couldn't find work there. They hoped life would be better in the city.

Naresh's home and family

Naresh lives in an area of Hyderabad called Peddamma Nagar. He lives with his mother, father, brother and sister. Their brick house has two rooms, a kitchen and a toilet. The floor is made of concrete and the house has a flat roof.

Naresh's family moved to Peddamma Nagar from the countryside where Naresh's father grew up. They moved because they had no jobs or land to grow crops on. However, life in the city is also hard. They have to pay for lots of things for the children, including school fees and clothes. Every week they also have to pay back a loan that they had to take out to pay for building their house. Sometimes the family has to pay for so many things that they do not have enough to eat.

Naresh's father works as a stonemason. He leaves home at 8am and cycles to work. He returns at 8pm. He works six days a week and has Sundays off. Naresh's mother stays at home and looks after the children. Lots of children in Peddamma Nagar do not go to school as their parents do not have enough money. Children often have to work to help bring money into the family.

Naresh's neighbourhood

In Peddamma Nagar things have improved recently. When Naresh's family first arrived here there were no toilets in the houses and no roads. Now, people tend to have their own toilets and there is a drainage system in the area. Down the road from Naresh's house there is a telephone booth and there are some shops selling food, household items and sweets.

If the family get ill they have to pay for medicine. They often go back to their village in the countryside to get medicine as it's much cheaper there. But for major illnesses, they use the private hospital. Although it is expensive, it is closer to their home.

Naresh's day

Naresh gets up at about 6.30am and his father takes him and his brother to school on his bike. School starts at 9.30am and he returns at 4pm. Naresh learns his subjects in English, even though he speaks a different language at home. At playtime he likes playing cricket with his friends.

Naresh's school, Little Star High School, has between 600 and 700 pupils with 35 to 40 in each class. The children don't have to wear a uniform if their parents cannot afford it.

Between 4pm and 5pm Naresh has a meal of rice with *dal* (lentils). He likes to play with small cards and play cricket with his friends. Between 5pm and 7pm he goes for extra tuition. After 7pm he does his homework from school and from his tuition. He doesn't like having so much homework to do!

Sometimes before and after school, Naresh looks after his brother and sister while his mother, Nagalakshmi, does housework. As they don't have taps in their house, she has to carry pots of water from the spring or the nearby water tank. She has to pay for some of the water.

Naresh's family is keen that their children go to school. Naresh's father wants his children to be able to read and get a good job. "I am educating them so they can do a better job," says Naresh's father. At the moment only the boys go to school. Naresh's father would like Naresh's sister, Ammu, to go to school if they can afford it.

Meet Elene, 8, from Ethiopia

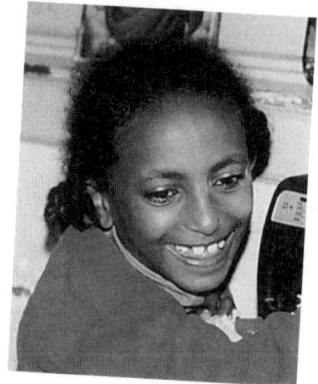

Elene lives in Addis Ababa, the capital of Ethiopia. This is an area where people who are poor and who are better off live close together.

Elene's home and family

Elene lives in an area of Addis Ababa called Taliyan Sefer. She lives with her mother, Amete, two brothers and three sisters in a two-roomed house made of *adobe* (mud). The roof is made of corrugated iron and there is an earth floor. They cook with wood and use charcoal to heat the house.

Elene's mother, Amete, prepares and sells a seed called fenugreek, which is used in cooking and herbal medicine and *besso* (roasted barley flour), which is used a lot in Ethiopian cooking. She buys the barley grain from the market, polishes it, roasts it and then grinds it. In addition to the cost of the barley, Amete has to buy wood for the fire. Her daughters help her cook food to sell, which adds to the family's income. Although the boys go to school, they also support the family by working in their mother's business when they can.

Elene's family are poorer than many other families in Taliyan Sefer. Some people in the neighbourhood have TV sets, sofas and CDs, but Elene's family have none of these. Elene thinks that the other children in the area are also better off than she is because they have fathers. Her father died five years ago. When he was alive, the family did not have problems, but since he died they have many problems. For example, they usually only eat two meals a day – they rarely eat breakfast.

Elene's neighbourhood

In Taliyan Sefer most of the houses are in poor condition. The narrow paths between the houses are often dirty and crowded. Most houses have no toilets and the residents have to share toilets. Despite this, Taliyan Sefer is not a slum area as people who are poor and those who are better off live side-by-side. Those who are better off tend to build high fences around their houses.

Being poor affects every aspect of Elene's life. Her family gets water from a nearby tap that other families also use. Elene's family also has to buy water. Her family cannot afford to see a doctor when they are ill as it is too expensive (a visit to the doctor costs about 20 birr, which is about £1.20); instead her family goes to a herbalist if they are ill.

Elene says her neighbourhood is dirty. People leave their rubbish in the streets, making a bad smell. Elene's mother does not like Elene to go out. Most of the time Elene plays indoors with her friends.

Elene's day

Elene goes to Arbegnotch school, which is a state school 1½km from her home. She is in Grade 3. She is clever and really enjoys school, particularly English.

Elene is disappointed that she only goes to school for half a day. Other children in the neighbourhood, who go to private school, attend for the whole day. Elene cannot go to private school because her family does not have enough money. It's even difficult for Elene's mother to pay the contributions for her school fees of 50 birr (about £3) a year.

When Elene gets home, she does her homework then plays games, such as hide-and-seek, with her friends. She helps around the house with washing the dishes and cleaning. When Elene grows up she wants to be a doctor. "There are not many rich people here, but I think most people in other countries are richer than us," says Elene.

Meet Alexia, 8, from Peru

Alexia lives in the rainforest in central Peru.

Alexia's home and family

Alexia lives in the rainforest in central Peru. She lives with her mother, Ruth, and her seven-year-old sister, Xiomara. They live in a one-roomed hut built of wood with a thatched roof. The hut has an earth floor and they use shared toilets. In this one-roomed house they cook, eat and sleep. In their home they have a radio but no TV. Alexia watches TV at friends' houses.

Alexia's uncle, Robin, lives next door with his family on their plot of land. Alexia's mother doesn't have any land of her own, so she works with her brother on his. There are orange trees growing on his land and they work to care for the trees and harvest the oranges when they are ripe.

Alexia's father doesn't live with them. He is separated from her mum and now lives in Lima. He comes to visit them from time to time.

Alexia's neighbourhood

Alexia lives in the rainforest. She feels that her neighbourhood is a safe place to live. She likes having so many plants and trees around – it means there are plenty of fruit and vegetables. When Alexia wants some fruit, she picks it from her uncle's land. However, as the family don't have much money, she doesn't always get enough of other types of food.

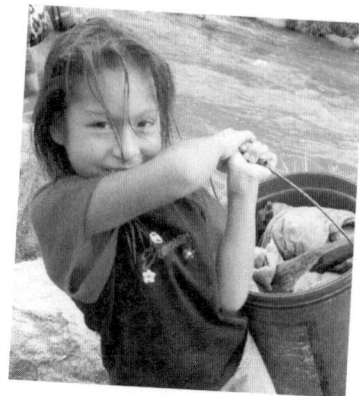

Alexia is also surrounded by many rainforest animals, although they tend to hide from people. These include monkeys, parrots, toucans, jaguars, tapirs and frogs.

Alexia's day

Alexia gets up at 6am and goes to the river to wash, get dressed and have breakfast. She goes to Chavini community school from 8am to 1pm. She speaks Spanish at school. At home she speaks a different language, Quechua.

The school is 1½km away. The road is very dusty, so Alexia and Xiomara sometimes go to school by taxi. Alexia is particularly good at sport and is in the school volleyball team. Her favourite subjects at school are maths, communications, science, personal well-being (PSHE) and religion (RE). She likes art – she often draws plants and flowers in her spare time.

After school, Alexia goes to the river to bathe with her sister and cousin, Fidel, who is seven. If the river is low it can be dangerous bathing because there are lots of large stones, but Fidel, Alexia and Xiomara know where the stones are, so they feel safe.

Sometimes, after school, Alexia does jobs around the house – making her bed, washing the dishes and helping her mum with other household chores, such as sweeping the patio. She also meets her friends to play volleyball, hide-and-seek and tag.

Education is important for Alexia and her family. Alexia would like to be a teacher when she grows up. Her mother makes Alexia do her homework – Alexia's mother never finished school because her family did not have enough money. "I hope my girls will study well and become somebody someday, better than me," says Alexia's mum.

5 Activities

Four children's lives from around the world

1–2 HOURS

Summary

This activity introduces the four children featured in the *Welcome to My World* pack.

Pupils first consider key elements of their own lives, gaining an understanding of the key geographical terms 'urban' and 'rural'.

After reading short descriptions of the four children's lives, pupils complete a table and use this to compare their lives with the four case study children.

Extension activities provide opportunities to explore further the children's lives and their countries.

Learning outcomes

- Pupils gain an understanding of the geographical terms 'urban' and 'rural'.

- Pupils compare the lives of four children living in less economically developed countries.

Preparation and resources

- Make one large copy of the world map on page 3.

- Make multiple copies of:
  Activity Master 1a (page 37)
  Activity Master 1b (page 38).

- Find two photos of a rural area in the UK and two photos of an urban area in the UK to show to the whole class.

Instructions

Let's start with me

1. Give out *Activity Master 1a*. As a whole class, answer the questions in the 'me' column of the table, introducing the key geographical concepts of **urban** and **rural**. Pupils either circle or underline the correct answer in the appropriate place in the table.

For question 1, put up the world map (page 3) and show pupils where the UK is. Point out key places in the UK and look at the position of the UK in Europe and the rest of the world.

For question 7, lead a discussion with the whole class on the differences between **urban** and **rural**. Display photos of rural and urban scenes in the UK that you have sourced before the lesson. Ask pupils which photo each of the following statements best describes:

- There are many buildings here.

- There are many shops here.

- You can probably walk to a shop to buy a pint of milk and a newspaper.

- You might have to drive to the nearest shop.

- You might find sheep and cows living here.

- You might find farmers living here growing crops.

- There aren't many trees here.

- There isn't much space here.

- There are many cars here.

- You might see tractors ploughing the fields.

2. Discuss which type of place pupils live in and the benefits and disadvantages of living where they do.

3. Once the pupils have completed the table about themselves, conduct a brief class discussion to outline the main similarities and differences between pupils' lives in the UK. They could consider the following questions:

   a. How many brothers and sisters do people tend to have?

   b. What sort of houses do people in the UK live in?

   c. What is the average number of people living in one house?

   d. Have pupils ever moved from one area to another? What are the similarities and differences between these areas?

Now let's meet Mai, Naresh, Elene and Alexia

4. Ask pupils to share examples of places they have been to by plane. Show the class where these places are on the world map. Ask pupils to imagine somewhere far away that they would go to by plane.

5. Explain that pupils are going to 'meet' four children – Mai, Naresh, Elene and Alexia – who live in four different countries. Complete the first line of the table as a whole class activity, pointing out on the world map where each of the four children lives.

6. Give out *Activity Master 1b*. Ask pupils to read through the brief descriptions of the four children's lives and then complete the rest of

the table. Alternatively, you could read out the descriptions on Activity Master 1b to the whole class and ask pupils to complete the table at the same time.

7. As a whole class, discuss similarities and differences between the four children, and between pupils' own lives:

- Do all children go to school?

- What are the benefits of going to school?

- Who has the most brothers and sisters?

- What are the benefits of having lots of brothers and sisters?

- What are the benefits of having no brothers and sisters?

- What are the different types of materials used to build houses?

- Who has the most rooms in their home?

- What are the problems of having only one room in your house?

- Why do people only have one room in their house?

- Who has the most people living with them?

- What are the benefits of having lots of people living with you?

- What are the problems of having lots of people living with you?

- Which children live in rural areas?

- What do you think are the benefits of living in a rural area?

- What are the disadvantages of living in a rural area?

- Which children live in urban areas?

- What do you think might be the benefits of living in an urban area?

- What are the disadvantages of living in an urban area?

- Where do you think the kitchen, bathroom and toilet are in a one-roomed house?

8. End the lesson by asking pupils to choose one of the children they have just been studying and to write a list of similarities and differences between themselves and the child.

Differentiation

With lower Key Stage 2 pupils, follow the same lesson as outlined above, but use *Activity Master 1a LKS2* and *Activity Master 1b LKS2* (pages 39 and 40). (*Note:* discussion of the differences between urban and rural life refers to question 5 of the table on *Activity Master 1a LKS2*, not question 7.)

Extension activities

- Ask pupils to write a paragraph about themselves in a similar format to those on *Activity Master 1b*.

- Ask pupils to choose one of the four children featured in the activity and to write a letter to them, telling them about their lives and asking them questions that they might want answered.

Using the country profiles (on page 16)

- Divide the class into groups and give each group a copy of each of the four country profiles. The groups could analyse each country profile and write down a list of how that country is similar to the UK.

- As a whole class, go through each country profile and discuss how similar or different each country is to the UK.

- Give each pupil one of the country profiles and ask them to use this information to design a fact file or web page about that country. Encourage them to find additional information from library books or the Internet.

- Divide the class into pairs and give out the country profile of the UK and one of the other country profiles to each pair. Pairs compare the two country profiles and write a paragraph on differences and similarities between the two countries. Then, as a whole class, consider what other information might give a more in-depth view of life in another country.

- As a whole class, compare and analyse the climate information at the end of each of the five country profiles (including the UK) to find out which place is the hottest, which is the wettest, which is the driest and which is the coldest.

- Ask pupils to look at the climate information at the end of the five country profiles (including the UK) and to consider what they might need if they were packing for a holiday to one of the non-UK countries. You may want to provide a list of items – sunglasses, umbrella, raincoat, sandals, boots, shorts, jumper, etc.

What are young lives like in the world?

Questions	Me	Mai	Naresh	Elene	Alexia
1. Where do you live?	UK Peru Ethiopia India Vietnam	UK Peru Ethiopia India Vietnam	UK Peru Ethiopia India Vietnam	UK Peru Ethiopia India Vietnam	UK Peru Ethiopia India Vietnam
2. Do you go to school?	Yes No	Yes No	Yes No	Yes No	Yes No
3. How many brothers and sisters do you have?	None 1 2 3 4 5 or more	None 1 2 3 4 5 or more	None 1 2 3 4 5 or more	None 1 2 3 4 5 or more	None 1 2 3 4 5 or more
4. What type of house do you live in?	Wooden Brick Concrete Mud	Wooden Brick Concrete Mud	Wooden Brick Concrete Mud	Wooden Brick Concrete Mud	Wooden Brick Concrete Mud
5. How many rooms are there in your house?	2 3 4 5 or more	2 3 4 5 or more	2 3 4 5 or more	2 3 4 5 or more	2 3 4 5 or more
6. How many people live in your house (including you)?	2 3 4 5 6 7 or more	2 3 4 5 6 7 or more	2 3 4 5 6 7 or more	2 3 4 5 6 7 or more	2 3 4 5 6 7 or more
7. What type of settlement do you live in?	Rural (countryside) Urban (town/city)	Rural (countryside) Urban (town/city)	Rural (countryside) Urban (town/city)	Rural (countryside) Urban (town/city)	Rural (countryside) Urban (town/city)

Save the Children   Young Lives
An International Study of Childhood Poverty

Meet Mai, Naresh, Elene and Alexia

Hello! My name is Mai.
I am ten years old. I live in Nam Cut village in Vietnam. I live in a one-roomed wooden house with my parents, younger sister, baby brother, grandmother and grandfather.
I go to school every day.

Hi! My name is Naresh.
I am nine years old. My father, mother, little sister, and little brother stay in this house. I live in Hyderabad which is a big city in India. My house has two rooms and is made from brick.
I go to school every day.

Hello! My name is Elene and I'm eight years old. I live in Addis Ababa, the capital city of Ethiopia. I live in a two-roomed house made from mud. I live with my mum, two brothers and three sisters. I go to school every day but not for the whole day.

Hi! My name is Alexia and I am eight years old. I live in a village in the rainforest of Peru. My house is a one-roomed hut built of wood. I live here with my mum and sister. I go to school every morning.

Save the Children   Young Lives

What are young lives like in the world?

Questions	Me	Mai	Naresh	Elene	Alexia
1. Where do you live?	UK Peru Ethiopia India Vietnam	UK Peru Ethiopia India Vietnam	UK Peru Ethiopia India Vietnam	UK Peru Ethiopia India Vietnam	UK Peru Ethiopia India Vietnam
2. Do you go to school?	Yes No	Yes No	Yes No	Yes No	Yes No
3. How many rooms are there in your house?	2 3 4 5 or more	2 3 4 5 or more	2 3 4 5 or more	2 3 4 5 or more	2 3 4 5 or more
4. How many people live in your house (including you)?	2 3 4 5 6 7 or more	2 3 4 5 6 7 or more	2 3 4 5 6 7 or more	2 3 4 5 6 7 or more	2 3 4 5 6 7 or more
5. What type of settlement do you live in?	Rural (countryside) Urban (town/city)	Rural (countryside) Urban (town/city)	Rural (countryside) Urban (town/city)	Rural (countryside) Urban (town/city)	Rural (countryside) Urban (town/city)

Meet Mai, Naresh, Elene and Alexia

My name is Mai.
I live in Vietnam. My house has
one room. Seven people live here.
I go to school every day.

My name is Naresh.
I live in India. My house has
two rooms. Five people live here.
I go to school every day.

My name is Elene.
I live in Ethiopia. My house has
two rooms. Seven people live here.
I go to school every day.

My name is Alexia.
I live in Peru. My house has one room.
Three people live here. I go to school
every morning.

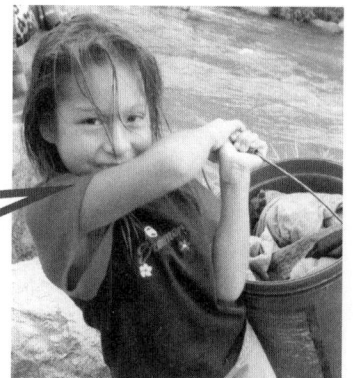

Save the Children   Young Lives
An International Study of Childhood Poverty

ACTIVITY 2

What's it like growing up in rural Vietnam?

1 HOUR

Summary

This activity looks at life for Mai, a 10-year-old girl living in a remote rural area in Vietnam.

Pupils briefly document what they do in a typical day. They then find out about Mai's life by watching a short film and reading her case study.

Pupils compare their typical day with Mai's.

Learning outcomes

Pupils find out about the daily routine of a child living in rural Vietnam.

Pupils feel empathy with that child.

Preparation and resources

- Make multiple copies of:
  Activity Master 2 (page 43)
  Mai's story (pages 26–27).

- Show the film about Mai from the DVD.

Instructions

Let's start with me

1. Give out *Activity Master 2*. Ask pupils to think about what they do at different times of an average school day and to complete the left-hand column of the table on *Activity Master 2*. As well as briefly describing, you may want to give them the option of drawing quick sketches.

Now let's meet Mai

2. Show pupils the short film about Mai on the DVD. After that hand out copies of Mai's story (pages 26–27) and ask pupils to read the section called Mai's day. (Alternatively, you may prefer to read out the story aloud to the class.) Ask pupils to complete the table recording what Mai does at different times of the day. Encourage pupils to include as much detail as possible, using information from the film as well as the handout on Mai's story. For example:

- Where does Mai live? What country? What is the name of her village?

- What is the village like where she lives?

- What time does Mai get up?

- How does she get to school?

- What is Mai's school like?

- Does she have a school uniform?

- What do you think the weather is like?

- What clothes does Mai wear? What does she wear on her feet?

- Where does she do her homework in her house?

- What games does Mai like playing?

3. Ask pupils to read the rest of the sheet about Mai's story, and to add any other relevant information to the table. (Alternatively, you could read this aloud to the whole class.)

4. Divide the class in half. Arrange pupils into pairs or groups of three. Ask one half of the class to devise a mime where they act out what Mai does during the day. Ask the other half of the class to act out what they themselves do during a typical day. Each pair or group of three then performs their mime to the class, alternating a group from one half of the class with a group from the other half. Ask a pupil to call out the different sections of the day at the relevant points of each performance (or call this out yourself).

5. As a whole class, discuss the similarities and differences between Mai's day and their own:

- How are the days similar?

- How are the days different?

- What would you like about Mai's day?

- What would you dislike about Mai's day?

- When do you think is Mai's favourite time of day?

- When do you think is Mai's least favourite time of day?

Differentiation

For lower Key Stage 2 pupils:

1. Give out *Activity Master 2 LKS2* (pages 44–45) and explain that pupils are going to think about what they do on an average school day. They should think about what they do at certain times of the day and complete the Activity Master. Pupils could also draw a quick sketch in the boxes.

2. Show the short film about Mai from the DVD. Ask pupils to cut out the pictures in *Activity Master 2 LKS2* and arrange them in the order they happen in Mai's day.

3. Carry out stages 3 and 4 of the activity (see above).

Extension activities

- Ask pupils to write an account entitled "A day in the life of Mai".

- Carry out the same activity for any of the other three children's stories in the pack. Then, as a whole class, discuss the similarities and differences between these children's lives.

- Ask pupils to write a story about their own lives in the same format as the one used for the stories of the four children featured in this pack (pages 26–33).

What is life like in rural Vietnam?

What I do...	What Mai does...
In the morning	In the morning 
At lunchtime	At lunchtime 
In the afternoon	In the afternoon 
In the evening	In the evening 

Save the Children

Young Lives
An International Study of Childhood Poverty

What is life like where I live?

What I do...

In the morning

At lunchtime

In the afternoon

In the evening

What is life like in rural Vietnam?

What Mai does...

ACTIVITY 3

Why did Katie buy her mum a goat for Christmas?

1 HOUR

Summary

This activity looks at how projects can help people from poorer communities improve their lives, and how pupils can get involved. The specific example is of a goat loan scheme.

The teacher starts by talking about different scenarios involving people borrowing things. Pupils are then given statements about goat loan schemes, which they use to solve the mystery of why Katie bought her mum a goat for Christmas.

Learning outcomes

- Pupils discover how projects such as goat loan schemes can help poorer people living in developing countries.

- They discuss and debate the issue of overseas aid.

Glossary terms (see page 92)

Kid

Loan

Preparation and resources

- Make multiple copies of *Activity Master 3*, one for each group (pages 48–51).

- Cut out the statements on the copies of *Activity Master 3* and put each set of statements into a separate envelope.

- Divide the class into pairs or small groups.

Instructions

Let's start with me

1. For this activity, pupils first need to understand what a loan is. Set up some simple drama scenarios with pupils to explain the term. For example:

- Ajay asks Matthew if he can borrow a pen. Matthew agrees, but says Ajay must give it back when he has finished with it. Ajay uses the pen then gives it back to Matthew.

- Sally asks Holly to lend her some money. Holly agrees. She asks Sally to pay her back when she gets paid.

- James goes to the library and asks to borrow a book. The librarian tells James that the book must be given back in three weeks' time.

- Lucy needs to borrow some money to buy a car. She goes to the bank and asks the bank manager if she can borrow £2,000. The bank manager agrees and explains that she will have to pay the money back within two years.

2. Discuss briefly with the whole class why people take out loans.

Now let's think about goats

3. Divide the class into pairs or small groups and give each group an envelope of statements (cut out from *Activity Master 3*).

4. Write the following question on the board:

   Why did Katie buy her mum a goat for Christmas last year?

5. Tell pupils that they have to try to work out the mystery of why Katie gave her mum a goat for Christmas. Ask pupils to read the statements and sort them into a logical order so that they begin to tell a story – and begin to solve the mystery.

6. Now ask groups to write down an answer to the question, based on the story they have developed from the statements. If pupils need further clarification of how the goat loan scheme works, use ten toy goats or counters to show how the goats are loaned, how they multiply and how they are paid back to the goat loan scheme.

7. As a whole class, discuss the following questions:

   • Why are goats loaned to poor families?

   • Why might it be better to give a family a goat rather than food?

   • What different uses does a goat have?

   • How different might the family's life be in ten years' time?

   • Are there any problems with goat loan schemes?

Differentiation

For lower Key Stage 2 pupils simplify this activity by giving them less statements – photocopy the first section of *Activity Master 3* for both lower and upper Key Stage 2 pupils (pages 48–50), but the second section (page 51) for upper Key Stage 2 pupils only.

Extension activities

• Pupils visit the Save the Children 'Wish List' website for schools – www.savethechildren.org.uk/forschools/

   Ask them to imagine they have £100 to spend on Christmas 'Wish List' presents for their family. What would they buy, for who and why?

• They then produce a poster for 'Wish List' that explains how you can help improve children's lives by buying one of the gifts.

---

i Information for teachers: animal loan schemes

In many countries, crops form a staple part of many people's diet, but if these crops fail, livestock can provide a safety net. Owning livestock means that people have something they can sell or barter when times are hard, or when they need cash to pay school fees.

Buying an animal is often too much for many people, so organisations such as Save the Children fund schemes that provide animals for families. Under animal loan schemes, a family is loaned a goat, cow or sheep to look after. When the goat, cow or sheep produces an offspring, the family gives the baby animal back to the loan scheme. In doing this, the family pays off their original loan and the animal they were lent becomes theirs. The offspring is loaned to someone else and the process starts again.

Animal loan schemes have proved a cheap and sustainable way to help people in poor communities own their own livestock. In addition, animal manure is a good fertilizer for crops.

Katie buys a goat from Save the Children's 'Wish List' for her mum and dad for Christmas.

Katie's mum does not actually get the goat! Instead, her mum receives a gift card telling her that a goat is going to a child who really needs it.

The goat is delivered to a girl called Tigist. She lives with her aunt because her parents have died.

Having a goat means that Tigist is able to earn money for the family.

The goat given to Tigist is part of a goat loan scheme. Ten goats were given to the village in total.

Tigist has to pay off the goat loan. When the goat gives birth to a female kid, the kid is given back to the goat loan scheme. Now, Tigist's loan is paid off. The female kid is loaned to another child in the village.

People living in the area where Tigist lives depend on goats for their survival.

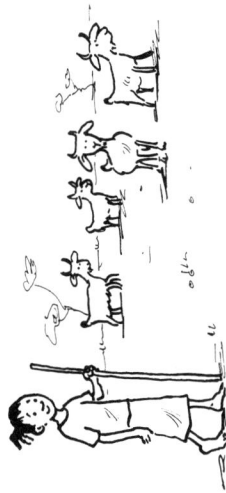

Tigist and her brothers and sisters have goat's milk to drink and to add to their porridge.

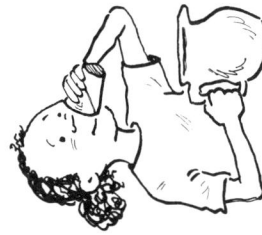

When the child's goat gave birth to a male kid, it was sold at the local market to buy clothes and pay for her to go to school.

Welcome to My World ACTIVITY MASTER 3 (3)

The goat kept on having kids and now the child owns a herd of ten goats!

Welcome to My World ACTIVITY MASTER 3 (4)

On special occasions, families kill a goat for meat.

Tigist was taught how to keep the goat healthy.

Goat manure – or goat poo – can be used as fertilizer to help the family's crops grow better.

The scheme also paid for the goat to have vaccinations (injections) to keep it healthy.

ACTIVITY 4

Why do people move from the countryside to towns and cities?

I HOUR

Summary

This activity explores why Naresh's parents moved from the countryside to the city.

Pupils first consider reasons why people in the UK move. They then tell the story of Naresh's father and mother by putting eight cartoon drawings in the right order.

Learning outcomes

Pupils have an understanding of migration from rural to urban areas and how it affects people and the environment.

Glossary term (see page 92)

Stonemason

Preparation and resources

- Make multiple copies of *Activity Master 4*, one for each group (page 54).

- Cut out the cartoons on *Activity Master 4* and put each set of cartoons into a separate envelope.

- Find the short film about Naresh from India on the *Welcome to My World* DVD.

- Divide the class into pairs or small groups.

Instructions

Let's start with me

1. As a whole class, discuss the terms 'rural' and 'urban'. Refer back to Activity 1. Talk about the area where pupils live.

2. As a whole class, discuss why people in the UK might want or need to move. Ask pupils why they or other members of their family may have moved. For example:

   - to move to a bigger house

   - to be near family

   - because their mother or father got a new job

   - to be in a more peaceful area.

Now let's consider Naresh

3. Explain to the class that you are going to show a short film about a boy called Naresh who lives in India in a city called Hyderabad. Write the following questions on the board:

   - Why did Naresh's parents move from the countryside to the city?

   - What is their house like?

   - What is the area like?

- What are the good things about living in this area?

- What are the problems of living here?

Before you show the film, ask pupils to read the questions and, when they watch the film about Naresh, to try to find the answers to those questions.

4. After showing the film, read out the case study of Naresh (page 28).

5. Give out *Activity Master 4* – a set of cartoon drawings – to the pairs or groups. Pupils should put the cards in the right order so that they tell the story of Naresh's parents moving from the countryside to the city.

6. As a whole class, discuss why Naresh's parents moved from the countryside to the city, and look at why other people move:

   - Why did Naresh's parents move from the countryside to the city?

   - What is life like where they live in Hyderabad?

- What is their house like?

- Do you think life is better for Naresh's parents in the city than it was in the countryside?

- Why do people move in this country?

- Do people move in this country for the same reasons as Naresh's parents?

- How might the environment be affected by people moving from the countryside to the city?

Differentiation

With lower Key Stage 2 pupils this activity can be carried out as a teacher-led activity, rather than pupils working in pairs or small groups.

Extension activity

Ask pupils to draw a cartoon showing what Naresh's life might have been like if he had stayed in the countryside.

This is the story of Naresh's dad, Srenu.

When Srenu was a boy, he lived in the countryside. He worked in the village fields with his brothers. He didn't go to school. His family was poor. Life was hard.

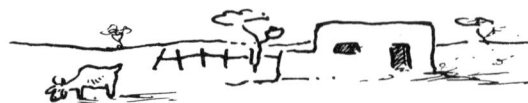

Srenu's brother, Ajay, found life hard in the countryside. He left the village and his family, including Srenu. Ajay went to the city of Hyderabad to find work. He got a job as a stonemason.

Srenu got married to Nagalakshmi. Life in the village was very difficult for them.

Srenu decided to follow his brother to Hyderabad. He and Nagalakshmi left the village.

When Srenu and Nagalakshmi arrived in the city they bought a tiny piece of land. Srenu got a poorly paid job as a stonemason.

Srenu and Nagalakshmi built a house on the land they had bought. It was a small brick house with two rooms plus a kitchen, a toilet and a bathroom.

Srenu and Nagalakshmi had three children, Naresh, Dotelawaprasad and Ammu. Srenu and Nagalakshmi wanted their children to get an education, but they could only afford to send Naresh and Dotelawaprasad to school.

Save the Children

Young Lives
An International Study of Childhood Poverty

ACTIVITY 5
What is Naresh's home like?

Summary

This activity helps pupils to get an idea of what it is like to live in a small house in the city of Hyderabad.

First, pupils consider what their houses are like. Then they make a model of Naresh's home.

Learning outcomes

Pupils empathise with Naresh and gain an understanding of what it is like to live in his house.

Glossary term (see page 92)

Rent out a room

Preparation and resources

- Project *Activity Master 5a* (plan of a typical semi-detached home in the UK – see page 57) and *Activity Master 5b* (plan of Naresh's home – see page 58) on a whiteboard or onto a wall.

- Make multiple copies of *Activity Master 5c* (pages 59–60) on card – one for each pupil.

- Scissors – one pair for each pupil or pair of pupils – and lots of glue or sellotape.

Instructions

Let's start with me

1. Show the plan of a home in the UK (*Activity Master 5a*) on a whiteboard or projected onto a wall. Pupils comment on how this plan is similar to or different from their home.

   - How many rooms are there in the house?

   - What is the main purpose of each room?

Now let's consider what Naresh's home is like

2. Show pupils Naresh's house plan (*Activity Master 5b*) on a whiteboard or projected onto a wall.

3. Tell pupils that they are going to make their own model of Naresh's house. First, demonstrate what you want them to do – ie, cut out a copy of *Activity Master 5c* and make it into a model. Once you have done the demonstration, give a card copy of *Activity Master 5c* to each pupil. Ask them to cut out their model and stick it together.

4. Ask pupils to put the Naresh figure into the model home. As a whole class, discuss the following questions:

   - How much space does Naresh's family have?

   - What problems do Naresh and his family face because they live in one room?

   - What are the good things for Naresh and his family about living in one room?

   - Why do you think the family rent out a room in their house?

   - Would you mind sharing a toilet with another family?

   - Where do you think the other family cook? (They don't share Naresh's family's kitchen.)

   - How similar or different is Naresh's home to your home?

   - How could Naresh's home be improved?

Differentiation

For lower Key Stage 2 pupils, enlarge *Activity Master 5c* to A3 and copy it onto A3 card. Ask pupils to work in pairs to make the model.

Extension activities

- Ask pupils to lay transparent squared paper over *Activity Master 5a* and *Activity Master 5b* to compare the difference in size between the two house plans.

- Map out Naresh's house in the school hall or playground, using chalk or string.

- Ask pupils to draw a plan of their own home.

- Ask pupils to make a card model of their home.

- Ask pupils to draw a map of their local area, showing all the places that are important to them.

- In the film on the DVD, Naresh says that if he had a lot of money he would buy clothes; flowers for his mother; flowers for his sister and shoes for his father. Ask pupils what they would buy for their family if they had lots of money. Discuss the differences between what they would choose and what Naresh said he would buy.

Plan of a typical semi-detached home in the UK

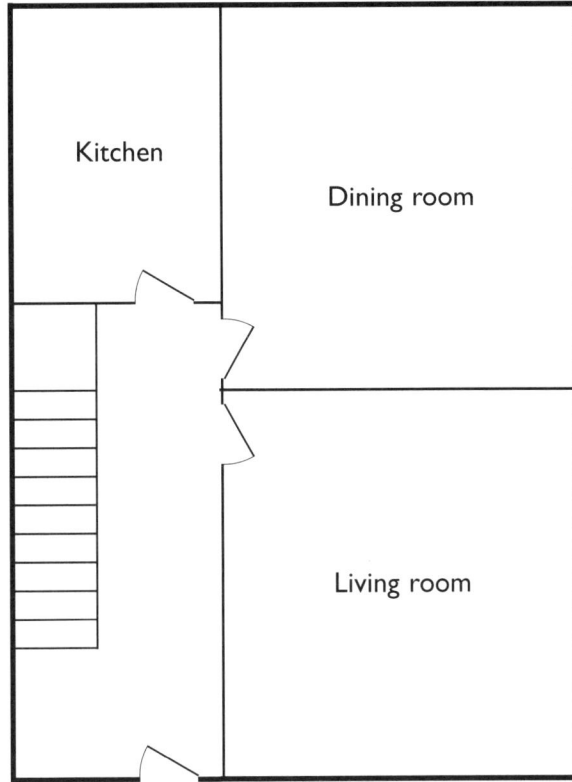

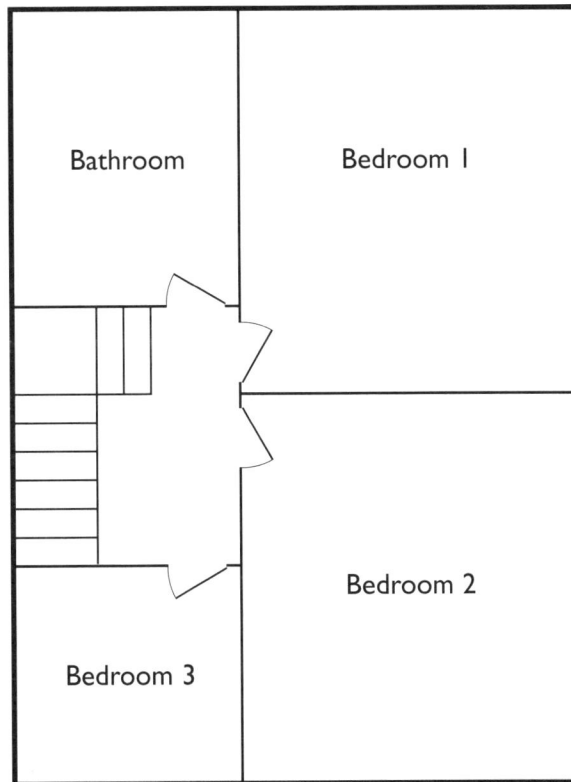

Kitchen

Dining room

Living room

Bathroom

Bedroom 1

Bedroom 3

Bedroom 2

0   1   2   3 metres

Save the Children   Young Lives
An International Study of Childhood Poverty

Plan of Naresh's home

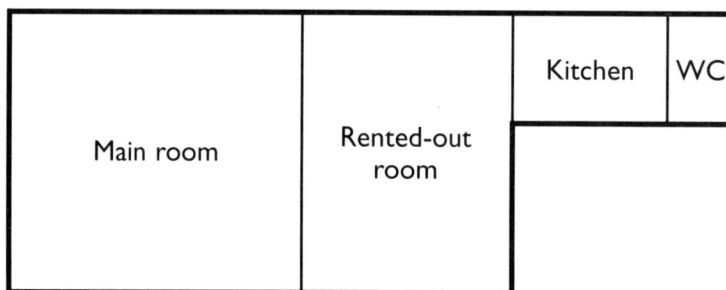

```
┌──────────────────┬──────────────────┬─────────────┬──────┐
│                  │                  │   Kitchen   │  WC  │
│                  │                  ├─────────────┴──────┘
│    Main room     │  Rented-out      │
│                  │     room         │
│                  │                  │
└──────────────────┴──────────────────┘
```

0   1   2   3 metres

Save the Children   Young Lives
An International Study of Childhood Poverty

Make a model of Naresh's home

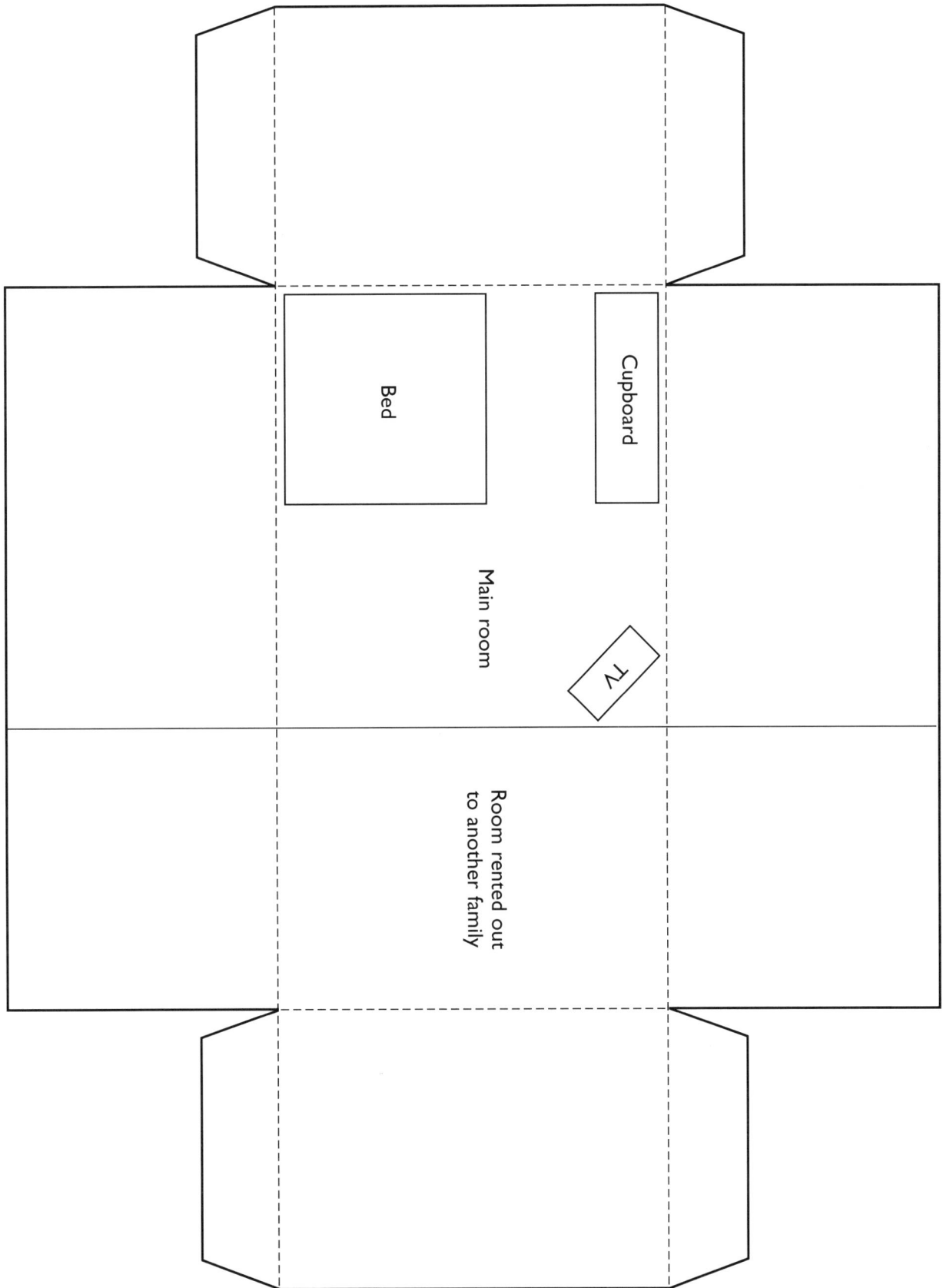

Bed

Cupboard

Main room

TV

Room rented out
to another family

0   l metre

Save the Children

Young Lives
An International Study of Childhood Poverty

Make a model of Naresh's home

Partition between main room
and rented out room

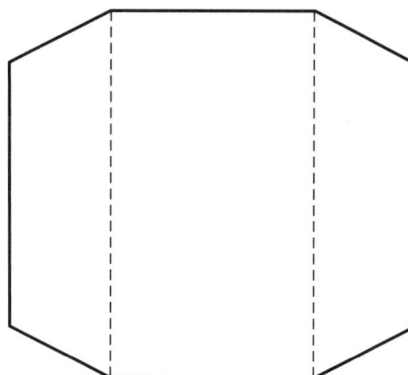

Partition between
kitchen and toilet

Fold on
dotted line

Scale person

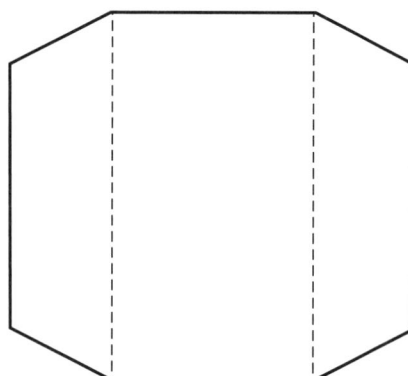

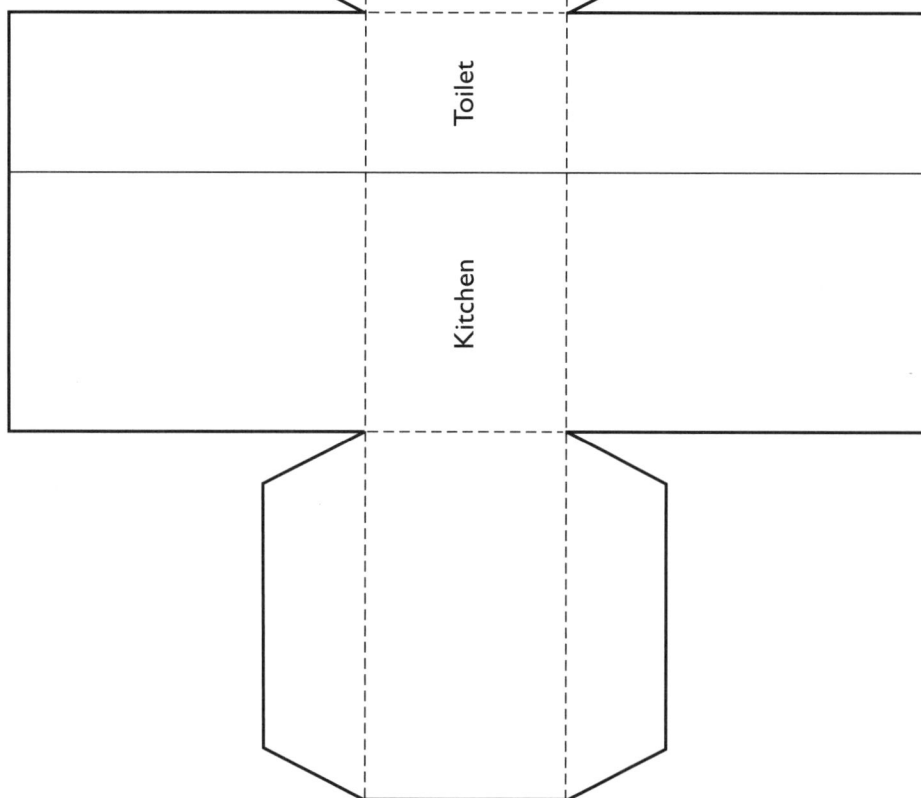

Toilet

Kitchen

0 | metre

Save the Children

Young Lives
An International Study of Childhood Poverty

ACTIVITY 6
What is Elene's local area like?

Summary

This activity looks at healthcare and, in particular, the importance of a clean environment.

Pupils consider the healthcare they can get and the environment where they live. They then look at healthcare and environmental health in the district of Addis Ababa, Ethiopia, where eight-year-old Elene lives.

Learning outcomes

- Pupils have some understanding of the importance of a clean environment in order to stay healthy.

- Pupils have some understanding of the healthcare available to Elene, a girl from a poor family in Ethiopia, and the health hazards in the district where she lives.

Glossary terms (see page 92)

Herbalist

Polluted river

Preparation and resources

- Make multiple copies of *Activity Master 6a* (the map on page 63) – one copy for each pair of pupils.

- Make multiple copies of *Activity Master 6b* (statements about the area where Elene lives on page 64) – one copy for each pair of pupils.

- Find the short film about Elene from Ethiopia on the *Welcome to My World* DVD.

Instructions

Let's start with me

1. Ask pupils a series of questions related to healthcare and environmental health:

   - When you are ill – for example, if you have a sore throat – what do you do?

   - If you broke your leg, what would you do? What would happen after that?

   - When you have finished with something, like a banana skin, what do you do with it? Then what happens to it? Where does our rubbish end up?

   - When you have finished with your bath water, what do you do? What happens to water that goes down the sink?

   - When you go to the toilet and pull the flush, where does it go? What happens to sewage?

   - When you want a bath, what do you do? How does water get to our homes?

2. Ask pupils to keep this information in their minds as they look at Elene's life.

Now let's think about Elene's health and environment

3. Explain to the class that you are going to show a short film about a girl called Elene who lives in the capital city of Ethiopia, which is called Addis Ababa. Write the following two questions on the board and ask pupils to think about them while they watch the film:

   - Where do people throw their rubbish?

   - When Elene is ill, where does she go?

4. Read out Elene's story to the whole class (page 30).

5. After the film, divide the class into pairs. Give each pair copies of *Activity Master 6a* (a map of Elene's neighbourhood) and *Activity Master 6b* (a set of statements about where Elene lives). Ask pupils to work in pairs to look at each statement on *Activity Master 6b*. They should then decide where each statement refers to on the map. Ask them to mark that place on the map with the number of that statement in the relevant circle on the map. (For example, they should write 'I' on the map where they think statement I will take place.) Some statements will not have one definite place on the map – pupils should aim for the most likely place or places.

6. As a whole class, discuss Elene's healthcare and environment:

   • What does Elene do when she gets ill? Is this similar or different to what you do when you get ill?

   • What happens to rubbish in Elene's area? Is this similar or different to what happens to rubbish in your area?

   • What does Elene do when she needs to go to the toilet? Is this similar or different to what you do when you need the toilet?

   • What does Elene do when she wants to have a wash? Is this similar or different to what you do when you want to have a wash?

Differentiation

For lower Key Stage 2 pupils, instead of *Activity Master 6b*, give pairs of pupils a copy of the simpler *Activity Master 6b LKS2* (page 65). This has a list of different places, along with a drawing of each of them. Pupils find each of these places on the map (*Activity Master 6a*), and write the number of each place on the map.

Extension activities

• Ask pupils to use the map and the information in the statements to write a diary entry called 'A day in the life of Elene', describing what Elene does during her day and all the places she visits.

• The map shows all the places that Elene considers important in her local environment. Ask pupils to produce a similar map for the area where they live, including all the places that they consider important.

Map of Elene's neighbourhood

Save the Children

Young Lives
An International Study of Childhood Poverty

What is Elene's local area like?

1. Elene lives here – in a one-roomed house made from dried mud. She lives with her mother, two brothers and three sisters.

2. These are the shared toilets. This is where Elene and her family have to go to the toilet.

3. This is where people go to see a doctor. It costs about 20 birr (£1.20) to see a doctor.

4. Elene's family cannot afford to see a doctor so she goes here to see a herbalist when she is ill. She buys herbs, takes them and then sleeps off the illness.

5. This is where Elene goes to school. She only goes for half a day. Her mother cannot afford to send her to private school, which lasts all day.

6. This is where people might go for a cup of coffee and a bite to eat. Elene's family do not go here as they do not have enough money.

7. This is where Elene's family go to collect water. Sometimes the water runs out and they have to buy water.

8. This is where Elene's neighbours throw their rubbish. It smells bad. Elene is not allowed to play outside because of the rubbish.

9. These are the houses where people with more money live. Their houses have high fences around them. These people have TVs, sofas and CD players.

10. This is where people go when they are really ill. Elene's family do not go here as they don't have enough money.

11. This river runs close to Elene's home. It is polluted and smells bad.

12. This is where some people wash their clothes.

13. This is where people go to church.

14. This is where people go to buy medicines. Elene's family cannot afford to buy medicines.

15. This is where Elene washes. She has no bath or shower. She uses a bucket of water.

What is Elene's local area like?

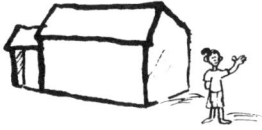

1. Elene's house

2. Shared toilets

3. Doctor's clinic

4. Herbalist

5. Elene's school

6. Café

7. Water tap

8. Rich person's house

9. Rubbish tip

10. The polluted river

11. The church

12. Chemist

ACTIVITY 7

How can Elene's local area be improved?

1 HOUR

Summary

Pupils consider how Elene's area could be improved.

Pupils review the ideas of the previous activity. They then consider the most appropriate ways to improve Elene's neighbourhood by carrying out a decision-making activity.

Learning outcomes

Pupils begin to recognise that local communities can improve their environment and the quality of people's lives.

Glossary terms (see page 92)

Work voluntarily

Employ someone

Water pump

Vaccinate

Preparation and resources

- Make multiple copies of *Activity Master 7* (page 68) – one copy for each pair or group of pupils.

- Make multiple copies of *Activity Master 6a* (page 63) – one copy for each pair or group of pupils.

- Divide the class into pairs or small groups.

Instructions

1. Begin by going over the previous activity (Activity 6). As a whole class, ask pupils to come up with a list of health problems that people in Elene's neighbourhood face. For example:

   - There is no rubbish collection in the area, so rubbish sits in the streets and people could catch diseases from it.

   - Families are too poor to visit a doctor, so diseases won't be cured.

   - The river has become polluted because factories and other people dump rubbish in it.

   - The river becomes polluted because people wash themselves and their clothes in it.

   - If people swim or wash in a polluted river, they may become ill.

2. Explain that a local charity has raised money to help improve people's health in Elene's neighbourhood. Give out copies of *Activity Master 7* to each pair or small group of pupils. Read aloud to the whole class the list of ideas on *Activity Master 7*, briefly explaining each idea.

3. Ask each group to discuss these ideas for improving people's health and to choose what they think are the three best ideas. Ask them to write down why they think these are the most useful in as much detail as possible.

4. Give each pair or group of pupils a copy of *Activity Master 6a* (map of Elene's neighbourhood). Ask them to mark on the map the three aid options they have chosen. For example:

- If they have chosen to employ more doctors, they should draw a few people next to the clinic.

- If they have chosen to put in a walled rubbish tip, they should draw this in a suitable place on the map.

- If they decide to vaccinate children, they could draw a sign saying 'vaccinate here' outside the school.

Differentiation

For lower Key Stage 2 pupils, this should be a teacher-led activity.

Extension activities

- Ask pupils to look at the website of Save the Children (www.savethechildren.org.uk) and to write a list of other ways Save the Children helps improve children's lives in developing countries.

- Ask pupils to research charities that work with children in the UK and to write a list of things these charities do to help improve children's lives in the UK.

How can the health of the people who live in Elene's area be improved?

A local charity has raised money to help improve healthcare in Elene's neighbourhood.

Choose the three ideas that you think would best help improve healthcare in Elene's area.

Ways to improve the health of the people who live in Elene's area	✓ Choose three
1. Build more toilets so that there is one toilet for every two families.	
2. Build a rubbish tip with a wall around it where people can dump their rubbish.	
3. Put in a water pump so that people don't have to buy water.	
4. Employ doctors from the UK to work voluntarily so that people don't have to pay to see a doctor.	
5. Give medicines to the health clinics so that people don't have to pay.	
6. Train people to become health workers so that they can teach people how to stay healthy – for example, by boiling water to kill any diseases or by keeping saucepans on a shelf and not on the floor.	
7. Clean up the river so that people can use it safely.	
8. Build more hospitals in the area.	
9. Employ nurses to visit schools and give basic healthcare, for example, checking for head lice.	
10. Make sure that children are vaccinated against some diseases.	

Reasons for your choices:

_____

_____

_____

ACTIVITY 8
What is Alexia's life like?

1 HOUR

Summary

Pupils find out about the day-to-day life of a girl called Alexia, who lives in the Peruvian rainforest. They watch a film about Alexia's daily life, and compare similarities and differences with their own lives.

Learning outcomes

- Pupils compare their day-to-day lives with the life of a girl living in the rainforest in Peru.

- Pupils empathise with aspects of her life, finding similarities as well as differences with their own lives.

Glossary term (see page 92)

Indigenous

Preparation and resources

- Make multiple copies of *Activity Master 8* (on page 70) – one for each pupil.

- Find the short film about Alexia from Peru on the *Welcome to My World* DVD.

Instructions

Let's start with me

1. Ask pupils to work in pairs to write a list of three things in their lives that they think are good and three things that they would like to change. As a whole class, ask pupils to call out the positive and negative things they have identified. Identify common themes.

Now let's meet Alexia

2. Give each pupil a copy of *Activity Master 8*. Then show the short film about Alexia from the DVD. While watching the video, pupils should decide whether each statement is true or false, circling the correct answer on *Activity Master 8*. You may need to play the film more than once or stop at appropriate places to help pupils complete this activity.

3. Read out Alexia's story to the whole class (page 32).

4. As a whole class, list on the board the good things and problems or bad things in Alexia's life. Ask the following questions:

- What are the good things about Alexia's life? Are these similar or different to the good things in your life?

- What are the problems in Alexia's life? Are these similar or different to the problems in your life?

- Are there any ways that Alexia's life could be improved?

Differentiation

For lower Key Stage 2 pupils, substitute *Activity Master 8 LKS2* (page 71) for *Activity Master 8*.

Extension activity

Pupils look at positive and negative aspects of the lives of one of the other children who appear in the *Welcome to My World* pack and DVD. They then compare this child with Alexia.

What is life like for Alexia?

Statements about Alexia's life	True or false?
1. Alexia gets up at 6 o'clock in the morning.	True / False
2. She washes in the river.	True / False
3. She does not go to school.	True / False
4. She does not have a television.	True / False
5. Her parents live together.	True / False
6. Alexia has to do household chores such as sweeping and making her own bed.	True / False
7. She is good at sports.	True / False
8. After school she plays in the river.	True / False
9. Alexia's mum did not finish school because her family did not have enough money.	True / False

Save the Children

Young Lives
An International Study of Childhood Poverty

What is life like for Alexia?

Statements about Alexia's life	True or false?
1. Alexia gets up at 6 o'clock in the morning.	True / False
2. She washes in the river.	True / False
3. She does not have a television.	True / False
4. She does not go to school.	True / False
5. After school she plays in the river.	True / False

ACTIVITY 9

What difference does education make to children's lives?

Summary

This lesson investigates how education affects children's lives. Pupils compare the lives of two imaginary children: Maria, who completed school, and Isabella, who did not. Pupils undertake a class activity with the teacher and then work in pairs to carry out a 'hot-seating' activity.

Learning outcomes

Pupils gain an understanding of how education can affect the quality of people's lives.

Preparation and resources

- Prepare *Activity Master 9a* (page 74) to use on a projector or draw a flowchart similar to *Activity Master 9a* on the whiteboard and enlarge the statements on *Activity Master 9b* (page 75) onto large pieces of paper.

- Make multiple copies of *Activity Master 9c* (page 76) – one for every two pairs or groups – and cut these up.

- Divide the class into pairs.

Instructions

Let's start with me

1. As a whole class, discuss the following questions about the value of education:

   - If children in the UK didn't go to school, what sort of jobs might they end up doing?

   - What sort of housing might they live in?

   - How much money would they have?

Now let's think about the difference education makes to children's lives in Peru

2. Ask the class to imagine they are meeting two 20-year-old young women from Peru: Maria, who has been to school, and Isabella, who has not. As a whole class, complete a flowchart for Maria and one for Isabella – pupils decide on a logical order for the statements on *Activity Master 9b* and fit them into the flowchart. Project the flowchart on page 74 onto the wall or draw a flowchart on the whiteboard, then stick enlarged statements from *Activity Master 9b* onto the flowchart.

3. Set up a 'hot-seating' activity. Divide the class into pairs or groups of three.

   Give half of the pairs or groups the **Journalist's brief: Interview questions for Maria** (from *Activity Master 9c*).

   Give the other pairs or groups the **Journalist's brief: Interview questions for Isabella** (from *Activity Master 9c*).

   In each pair or group, one pupil imagines that they are Maria or Isabella. The other pupil or pupils are interviewers.

   Start by modelling an interview with one pair or group in front of the whole class.

   Then ask pupils to carry out interviews in pairs or small groups.

4. Select volunteers to show their interviews to the class. Encourage pupils to comment critically on the answers given and to ask their own questions.

5. As a whole class, discuss the different outcomes of Maria and Isabella's life.

Differentiation

For lower Key Stage 2 pupils, reduce the number of questions that the pairs ask each other in the hot-seating activity.

Extension activities

- Ask pupils to write up the hot-seating activity as a radio script or a magazine article.

- Ask pupils to write a speech for pupils at Alexia's school to persuade them to work hard.

- Success can be measured in many ways. Write the statements below on the whiteboard, and then ask pupils to consider which of the following statements they think best measures how successful somebody is:

  - having good qualifications
  - having lots of money
  - having an interesting job
  - having a husband or wife or partner
  - having lots of designer clothes
  - having children
  - having a big house
  - having a fast car
  - being healthy
  - having lots of friends
  - being happy.

As a whole class, discuss why pupils made their choices.

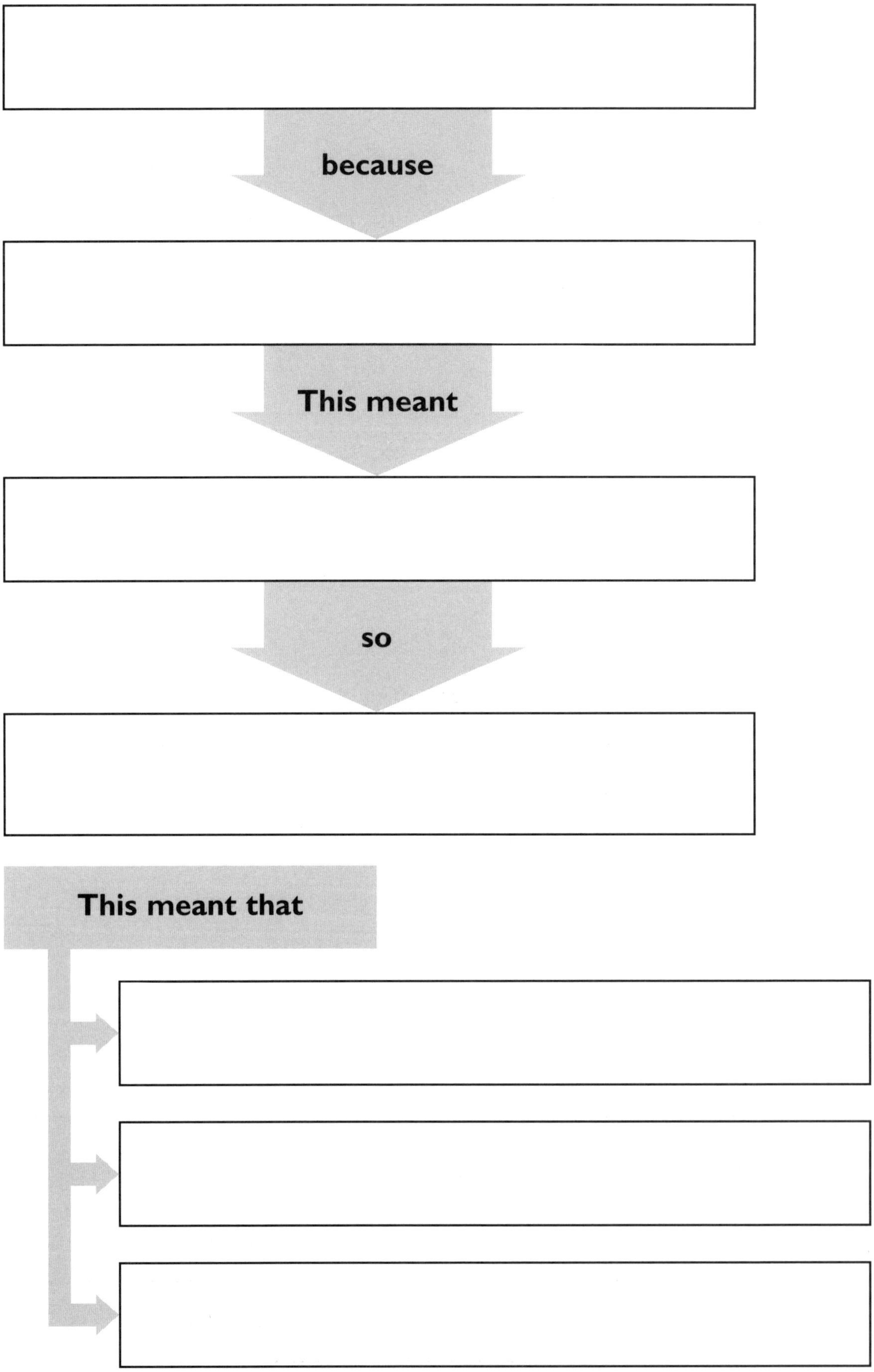
because
This meant
so
This meant that

Statements about Isabella

Isabella didn't go to primary and secondary school.
Her parents could not afford it.
She cannot read or write.
She could only get a poorly paid job.
She could only afford a small house in a poor area of town.
She could not afford to send her children to school.
She could not always afford to buy medicines.

Statements about Maria

Maria went to primary and secondary school.
Her parents were able to pay for her to go.
She passed all her exams.
She was able to go to college and then get a well-paid, interesting job.
She could afford to send her children to school.
She could afford a nice house.
She could afford to buy medicines.

Journalist's brief: Interview questions for Maria

Imagine you are interviewing Maria.

Maria's family managed to find the money to send her to school. She is now 20 years old.

Ask her some or all of the questions below to find out how school has helped her life.
Add your own questions.

What age did you start going to school?

Did you ever have times when you were not able to go to school? Why?

What did you enjoy about school?

What did you dislike about school?

What were your hobbies?

What job do you do now?

Has going to school helped you in your life? How?

How do you think your life might be different in ten years' time?

How different would your life be if you had not gone to school?

Journalist's brief: Interview questions for Isabella

Imagine you are interviewing Isabella.

Isabella's family did not have enough money to send her to school. She is now 20 years old.

Ask her some or all of the questions below to find out how not going to school has
affected her life. Add your own questions.

Did you ever attend school? If yes, when?

Why did you not go to school?

Can you read or write?

Were you happy about not going to school?

What did you do instead of going to school?

What job do you do now?

How do you think your life might be different in ten years' time?

How different would your life be if you had gone to school?

Save the Children

Young Lives
An International Study of Childhood Poverty

ACTIVITY 10

How can children's lives around the world be improved?

1 HOUR

Summary

This lesson explores ways in which children's lives can be improved – in the UK and in developing countries.

First, pupils consider where they can go if they need help. Then, they play a board game to see what types of support children in poor families in developing countries are likely to have.

Learning outcomes

Pupils recognise how people can improve their environment and how this can affect the quality of their lives.

Glossary terms (see page 92)

Pit latrine

Well

Environment

Hygienic

Housing co-operative

Sanitation

Preparation and resources

- Divide the class into pairs.

- Get 15 or more dice.

- Make multiple copies of *Activity Master 10a* (page 79) – one for each pair of pupils.

- Make multiple copies of *Activity Master 10b* (game cards and counters on pages 80–83) onto card – one for each pair of pupils. Cut out the counters and cards.

- Make multiple copies of *Activity Master 10c* (the game board on pages 84–85) onto card – one for each pair of pupils.

Instructions

Let's start with me

1. As a whole class, discuss the following question: 'If I need help, where do I turn?' Present different scenarios:

   - If there is a fire at my home, what happens?

   - If my house becomes flooded and lots of furniture is ruined, what happens?

   - If my mum or dad can't work, what happens?

   - If my uncle falls over at work and is injured and not able to work, what happens?

   - If my family can't afford to buy a home, what happens?

2. Explain to pupils that many developing countries cannot afford to provide the same kind of support that families get in the UK. For example:

   - Many families build their own homes.

   - If someone's house burns down, they have to rebuild it themselves.

   - If there is a flood and a family's furniture is ruined, they have to buy it again or do without.

   - If the father or mother in a family can't get any work, there is no income support.

   - If someone is injured at work, there are no benefits. The family has to do without their income.

Now let's consider how children's lives can be improved

3. Explain to pupils that they are going to play a game. To play the game, they need to imagine that they are a child living in a developing country. Read out the profile of this child to

the whole class (*Activity Master 10a*). Ask pupils to write a list of problems faced by the child. Give pupils a copy of this profile so they can refer to it as they play the game.

4. Give out copies of the board game to each pair of pupils. Ask them to lay out the differently shaped cards in the appropriate places on the board.

5. Explain that the aim of the game is to pick up one card for each of the four boxes on the board: school, water and sanitation, health, housing and environment.

6. Ask pupils to place their counter on the **'start here'** box on the board. They then take it in turns to throw the dice and move forward the number of spaces shown on the dice. When pupils land on one of the four boxes (school, water and sanitation, health or housing and environment) they pick up a corresponding card. For example, if the pupil lands on the school box they should pick up a school card. Once a pupil has got a card for one box, they cannot pick up another for the same box.

The game ends when one of the players has collected four cards, one from each box. Alternatively, you may prefer to set a time limit on the game, with pupils seeing how many cards they can get in a short amount of time.

7. After the game, pupils put the cards on the table in front of them. Using the profile of the child (*Activity Master 10a*), ask pupils to write a short paragraph of what that child's life is like now. If any pupils did not get any cards, they should use the cards of the pupil they were playing with.

8. End the lesson by discussing as a whole class the main outcomes for the child in the profile:

• How was the child's school life improved?

• How was the child's housing improved?

• How was the child's environment improved?

• How was the child's health improved?

• How was the child's access to water improved?

• How was the child's sanitation improved?

• What were the best improvements?

• How realistic is this game?

• Do you think the lives of all children from developing countries are like this? Take some time to discuss this with the whole class. Emphasise that children's lives are very varied in terms of wealth, housing, environment, services, etc.

Differentiation

For lower Key Stage 2 pupils you may want to play the game as a class activity with one pupil at the front of the class rolling a large dice, one pupil moving the counter and other pupils reading out the cards as required.

Extension activities

• Pupils could complete a brief evaluation of the work they have carried out over the *Welcome to My World* scheme of work. They could write down some or all of the following:

  – The child that I think has a life most similar to mine.
  – The child that I think has a life most different to mine.
  – Things that surprised me while I was learning about children around the world.
  – What I think life is like in Vietnam / India / Ethiopia / Peru.
  – What I would still like to know about life in these countries.

• The class or school could get involved with a fundraising activity to raise money for Save the Children. For ideas on fundraising activities, see pages 86 and 87.

A hard life

You are an eight-year-old child who lives in a poor village in a developing country. Every morning you have to walk four miles to collect water from a river – two miles there and two miles back. This takes a lot of time and means you do not have time to go to school all day. Also, your family is poor and can only afford to send you to school in the afternoons. The school is in the nearest town.

You live in a wooden hut which your family built. There is only one room where you all live and when it rains the roof leaks and you get wet. You have no toilet in your house and have to use shared toilets. These flood when it rains a lot and are often dirty. You often go hungry as your family cannot always afford food. When you get ill, your family cannot always afford to buy medicines. It is five miles to the nearest clinic or hospital.

Play the game to see how your fortune changes as different people and organisations give you and your family help!

Save the Children   Young Lives
An International Study of Childhood Poverty

Counters

Cards

Save the Children builds a well in your village. This means you don't have to travel four miles to collect water.

Water Aid builds a number of pit latrines in your village. One is built outside your house so you can go to the toilet easily and in a hygienic place.

Save the Children provides hygiene education which teaches your family how to be healthier, eg, boiling water before drinking it, washing vegetables before eating them.

The government installs a network of water pipes, which means that you now have water in your house. You no longer have to walk miles to collect water.

The government cleans up the river. This means you collect cleaner water for washing and drinking.

Save the Children
builds a school in your
village. This means that you do
not have to travel far to get to school
and can go for longer.

The
government
provides free primary
education for all. This means
that you can go to school every day,
all day. You can only go in the afternoon
though as you still have to collect water.

Save the Children
builds a library in your school.
This means you can borrow books
to read at home, which helps you
to read better.

A charity
called ActionAid
sponsors you to go to
school. This means your family
does not have to pay school fees.
You can only go in the afternoon though
as you still have to collect water.

Save the Children
provides free school books
and pens, which means that your
family does not have to spend so much
money to send you to school.

Save the Children sets up a work scheme in your village. This provides your dad with work, improving aspects of life in your village. This means you have more money coming in. You can afford more food and are no longer hungry.

Some adults in your village get together to form a housing co-operative. They all work together on one house, improving it, making it a bit bigger and making sure it doesn't leak. When they have finished, they move on to another house until all the houses in the village have been improved.

Save the Children's Wish List scheme provides your village with a loan of a goat. This goat provides your family with milk, which keeps you healthier. You hope that soon the goat will have baby goats, which you can eat or sell to make money.

Your father finds a better job which pays more. With the extra money, he buys some basic materials and improves your house. This means it doesn't leak when it rains.

Your mother is trained as a hygiene educator by Water Aid. This means that she is earning money for the family. This helps to buy more food and to pay for school fees.

Save the Children   Young Lives
An International Study of Childhood Poverty

The government cleans up the local rivers and streams in your area and forbids any businesses from dumping rubbish or chemicals in there. You find that you are ill less often after you wash in the river.

A group of UK volunteers come to your village and build a health clinic. This means you don't have to walk five miles for treatment when you are ill. However, your family can't afford to pay for treatment; you only use the clinic for emergencies.

The Rotary Club has provided glasses for your village. You need glasses and are given a pair, which means that you can work more quickly at school and learn more.

The government provides your village with free vaccinations for basic diseases. This means you are more likely to stay healthy.

One of Save the Children's UK campaigns has meant that you no longer have to pay to go to the doctor. You also don't have to pay for medicines. This means you stay healthier.

Start here

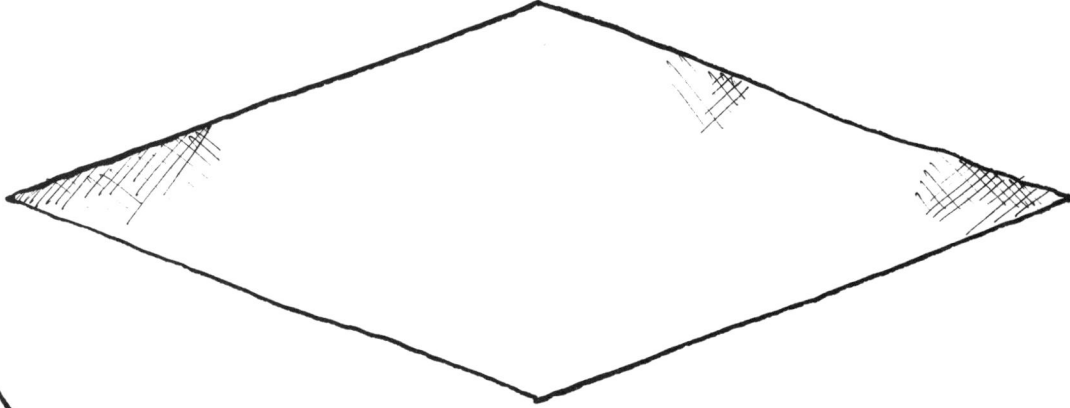

School

Housing and environment

Health and sanitation

Water

i Get involved! Fundraising ideas

Dress down day
Pupils donate to wear their own clothes rather than school uniform for a day. Teachers could join in the fun by wearing school uniform!

Fancy dress day
Pick a theme and make a donation to come to school in fancy dress. The theme could be famous celebrities or cartoon characters, or based on characters from history or English lessons.

Lunchtime jukebox
Make a donation to listen to your favourite songs at lunchtime.

Summer fête
Organise a summer fête or barbecue and invite the local community to come along and help fundraise with a bring-and-buy sale, cake sale, raffle and fun activities – like throwing wet sponges at teachers!

Concert/talent show
Put together a concert or talent show and sell tickets to other classes and teachers, as well as parents and other people you know.

Treasure hunt
Organise a treasure hunt where pupils donate to participate in the hunt for some great prizes. Don't forget to have a few booby prizes as well!

Art exhibition/sale
Put together an art exhibition of pupils' best artwork and invite parents and members of the local community to donate to view and/or buy the work. You could even hold an auction and sell the artwork to the highest bidder.

Sponsored challenges
Individuals, classes or the whole school can take part in sponsored challenges. You could hold a sponsored silence, a sponsored walk, a sponsored swim, a sponsored 'eat no sweets day'… the possibilities are endless!

Cake sale
Everyone bakes a cake or some biscuits and brings them into school to sell to other pupils and teachers at break time.

Board game tournament
Organise a board game tournament with all your favourite games – Monopoly, Cluedo, Chess, Pictionary… Pupils make a donation to play. The winner gets a prize.

Coins in a jar
Fill a jar with coins and ask pupils to donate to guess how many are inside. The winner gets a prize.

Sports challenges
There are all sorts of fun sports challenges. Pupils make a donation to take part in team games like netball and football, or to race in a three-legged race or a wheelbarrow race. You could even add a twist and do it all in fancy dress!

Celebrity quiz
Put together some questions about famous stars. Ask pupils and teachers to donate to enter the quiz. It could be played individually or in teams, or even one class against another. The winners get a prize.

i Celebrate global friendship through School Link from **Save the Children**

Sign up your school to School Link and:

- get access to FREE interactive resources to help teach about real life in a school in another country

- find out about children's lives through their own words

- get access to schemes and lesson plans linked to the primary curriculum

- take part in Friendship Friday, a creative fundraising day that allows pupils to make a difference to the lives of children and communities, like those that they have been learning about.

Find out more at
www.school-link.org.uk

i School speakers

Save the Children has a network of volunteer speakers across the UK who deliver talks to children about our work. Using children's stories and photos, the speaker brings alive the work that we do. Having a talk from one of our speakers is a great way of raising awareness about key issues that affect children in the UK and worldwide, and can support various aspects of the school curriculum. To find out whether there is a speaker available in your area, please contact our supporter care team on 0845 606 4027.

Speaking Out

i Wish List

Choose a gift from Save the Children's Wish List and we'll send it to children living in one of the poorest places in the world.

- Take the decision to make some wishes come true.

- Plan and carry out some fantastic fundraising activities.

- Choose your gift from a range of presents and send us your order form.

- We ensure your present arrives and that children's lives are changed for the better.

Find out more and download Wish List resources and order forms at
www.savethechildren.org.uk/forschools

Appendix 1: Film transcript

Mai
Lao Cai, Vietnam

Mai: My name is Doan Thi Mai. I am ten years old. I live with my grandparents and parents, and my younger brother aged two, and younger sister aged three.

Father: My main job is being a farmer, but the farming conditions are difficult. We have little land and don't grow any cash crops. The total income from our crops and carpentry is about 4 million dong a year.

Mai: Every morning I get up at 5.30am. I clean my teeth and face, have breakfast and go to school until 11.00am.

Teacher: Our school is classified as a 'Zone 3' school, because it is in a difficult area. So on top of family contributions, we get extra support from government for notebooks, text books and stationery.

Most people understand the importance of education.

The school is centrally located so children can get to school easily, but they don't live far away so the distance to school is not great. No child lives too close or too far away.

Mai: I come back home around mid-day, and have lunch. After lunch I rest from 12.00 noon to 1.30pm, and then go to graze the cows.

I come back at about 5.30pm.

After dinner I study by myself until 9.00pm. Then I go to bed until the next morning when I go to school again.

Mother: We live in difficult situations. I have to earn money to pay school fees.

At the beginning of the year we had no money, so we had to borrow money at 1 per cent interest.

If we have nothing to sell, we borrow to pay for school maintenance, books and other things, so she can go to school.

Mai: I want to be a doctor so that I can help sick people.

Naresh
Hyderabad, India

Naresh: My name is Naresh. I am nine years old. My father, my mother, little sister and little brother stay in this house. My father's name is Srenu, my mother's name is Nagalakshmi. My sister's name is Ammu; my brother's name is Dotelawaprasad. All of us live here.

Srenu, Father: I came here 15 years ago as a bachelor. After I got married I am here with my family. In my childhood I used to work in the village fields. My brothers worked here in Hyderabad as masons. My mother wanted me to join them. That's how I came to Hyderabad. Earlier I stayed with my brother, but after getting married, we came here.

Nagalakshmi, Mother: We felt bad leaving our village; even our parents felt bad. We had nothing there for our livelihood, so we came here. We borrowed money and built this house.

Srenu, Father: Although we took a loan of only 10,000 rupees, the interest is very high. We have managed to pay back only the interest because of expenses on the children.

We are somehow struggling to educate them. I'm able to run the house only if I work every single day. We are uneducated; if our children remain uneducated then, for example, the letter you sent us along with the photographs – somebody else had to read it for us. That's why I'm educating my children at all costs.

Q: What do you like in your school?

Naresh: I like my friends. I like Prawina, my teacher. She is teaching nicely. I don't have to read the text books. She writes on the board. We copy that on the slates. She writes in English. Dog. Fan.

Q: Do you know the spellings?

Naresh: [Recites spellings]

Q: Have you observed any difference between the growth of your daughter and your earlier children?

Nagalakshmi, Mother: We did not have to spend much money on the older children, but for this child we have spent a lot on hospitals.

Q: What happened?

Nagalakshmi, Mother: She often gets a cold, cough and fever, every two days, even now.

She plays a lot when her father is around – keeps saying, "Daddy, Daddy". She's also happy with her brothers. She brightens up around them.

Q: Do you like to play with her?

Naresh: Yes I do.

Q: What does she like to play with you?

Naresh: Any game. She follows me around.

Srenu, Father: We will educate her as much as we can, but we can't educate her enough to get a job. We will keep her in school until the 7th or 8th grade, and then maybe teach her something like tailoring. And then we will find her a good match in our community, and get her married.

Q: If you had a lot of money, what would you like to buy for your mother and father and your little sister?

Naresh: I would buy clothes. Flowers for my mother, and flowers for my sister.

Q: And for your father?

Naresh: My father – shoes.

Elene
Addis Ababa, Ethiopia

Elene: My name is Elene and I'm eight years old. Everyone in this neighbourhood is rich. They have TVs, sofas and CDs. I don't. All the kids around here attend school the whole day, but I only go to school for half a day because we don't have enough money.

This is a smelly neighbourhood. People from other neighbourhoods dump their garbage here. It stinks. My mom never lets me play outside. She says I'll get sick and maybe even catch malaria. So I never go out.

When I'm sick, I never go to the doctor. I just take my herbs, cover myself up, go to sleep and I get better.

It's been almost four years since my father died. When my father was alive, we never had problems. Now, I have no idea where my mom gets food or money.

If there's food we eat; if not we survive on roasted peas.

I have two brothers and three sisters; I'm the youngest. I like my brothers and sisters, but my mom is my favourite. When I grow up, I won't marry. I'll just help my mom.

Alexia
Central Peru

Alexia: I get up at 6.00am. I go and wash in the river. Then I have breakfast and get changed, and then go to school.

Then I come home, have lunch, I watch a little TV and go to bed.

Mother: After Alexia was born, when she was a baby, my mother took care of her. I left her with my mother until she was seven months old, then I went to Lima. When she was 11 months old, I asked for her to come to Lima.

There she celebrated her first, second and third birthdays. Then we returned, and that's when I began having problems with her father. We separated and ever since then I have lived alone here.

Alexia: Sometimes when mum is cooking, I make my bed. After cooking, I wash the dishes.

I sweep, I get up early and sweep this patio, then over there, then my aunt's patio.

Mother: Even though her father sends child support, it's not enough. I don't use firewood. I cook with kerosene. And to pay for this I have to pick oranges and help with the harvest, to get the money.

Alexia: My dad is Nono Caseos. He works on the trucks. He loads cocoa, coffee and cement. Right now, I think he's in Lima. Sometimes he comes here. We don't play. He sleeps.

He sleeps, has lunch, goes back to bed.

He stays two or three days, then leaves.

Teacher: Here at the Chavini school most children are settlers, with the exception of Alexia, who is Nomatsiguenka. Sometimes when they see you, the indigenous people hide or run off. Alexia's mother isn't like that. I guess that's why she sent her to this school.

Mother: In the old days, grandparents, they couldn't sign their names. They were afraid of the settlers. In a modern world, children have to learn a little at least, to be something.

Teacher: In the classroom she is very restless, active and communicative. She stands out above all in sports. Considering her mother is Nomatsiguenka, she's managed to adapt in a short time. Now it's as if she were any other child.

Mother: I can't make her be something, she has to choose what to study. If she wants to be a teacher, like she says, or a nurse, that's her goal. We can't force her.

Her dad wants her to study. He wants to take her to study in Lima.

I make her do her homework, so that she'll be better – better than her mother.

I didn't finish school, because we didn't have money.

Appendix 2: Glossary of terms

Aid: help given by the richer countries of the world to the poorer ones. For example, giving medicines after an earthquake.

Employ someone: give someone a job.

Environment: everything around us – everything we touch, smell, see and hear.

Herbalist: a traditional doctor who gives herbal remedies (plants) to people to make them better.

Housing co-operative: people working together to improve housing.

Hygienic: when something is clean and free from germs. If things are hygienic then you are more likely to stay healthy.

Indigenous: people who have always lived in a particular place, eg, rainforest.

Kid: a baby goat.

Loan: person A gives money/goods to person B; person B must then pay person A back at a later date.

Pit latrine: a large hole dug in the ground with a large piece of wood/metal over the top where people can go to the toilet.

Polluted river: a river that is dirty from having rubbish or chemicals in it.

Rent out a room: to give someone a room to live in, at a cost.

Sanitation: the disposal of sewage (toilet waste) and rubbish from homes.

Stonemason: a person who cuts, prepares and builds with stone.

Vaccinate: to give an injection to protect against diseases.

Water pump: a device to get water out of the ground.

Well: a deep hole in the ground where people can get water. You lower a bucket down to collect the water.

Work voluntarily: to work for no money.